HOW TO STOP BEING A NARCISSIST

The Complete Guide to Stop Controlling People, Stop Being Abusive, and Fix Your Relationships

JAMIE WILLIAMS

OAKRIDGE PRESS

CONTENTS

INTRODUCTION

If you do not change direction, you might end up where you are heading. —Lao Tzu

As someone who recently noticed how your toxic traits damage important relationships in your life, it is time to change direction so that you avoid causing more harm. In order to fix and improve broken relationships, you need to focus on becoming a better version of yourself. Here's the big question: Are you willing to change direction or stay on the route leading to destruction? In this moment, it is easy to choose the former and make the conscious decision to move in a different direction that will eventually lead to greener pastures but truth be told putting in the work to get there won't be easy.

Knowing you are the one who messed up a relationship, whether it was with a romantic partner you saw a future with, your child, sibling or cousin, it stings. It pushes you to go inward and ask yourself, *Why do I behave like I do, why do I say the things I say, why do I keep damaging my relationships*? Sometimes getting the answers while doing introspection doesn't come easily. But with time, patience, keeping an open-mind, and being honest with yourself, the answers will reveal themselves. You may not be aware of how certain habits and traits you possess affect your relationships, you have a different way of showing love, maybe you are dealing with trauma or painful memories stuck in your nervous system that negatively affects how you come across to others. This means you need to unlearn certain toxic traits and habits as well as restructure your mind for a healthier version of you to emerge so that healthier and long lasting relationships could follow. The question "Why do I have to change myself for others?" might pop up during your journey of getting rid of toxic and unwanted traits, but you need to remember the end goal: fixing your damaged relationships and attracting better future relationships by being a better you.

In this book, six topics will be covered. First, we look at the narcissistic spectrum and what causes people to develop narcissistic tendencies. After you learn about the ins and outs of narcissism, you will be introduced to five different methods that will help you improve your narcissistic behaviors. Let's look at a few benefits of this book:

- Increases your level of self-awareness
- Helps you get to know yourself on a deeper level
- Encourages you to work on improving yourself
- Teaches you methods that can be used to unlearn bad habits
- Helps you to rewire the brain for positive connections and for a better version of yourself to arise
- Allows you to work on yourself at your own pace without going to therapy sessions

This book encourages and motivates you to be accountable, and to develop a sense of safety within your own skin. When we feel unsafe or detect danger our brains respond on our behalf, which means we have less control over our conscious mind, leading us to do things we later regret. Only when we feel safe in our own bodies will our decision-making skills, self-love, and how we treat the ones around us improve. Most times we are vulnerable and act out in ways that are unhealthy to the self, as well as significant others, family, friends and colleagues. We unintentionally hurt the ones we love the most because we are uneducated in how to respond to our emotions. However, you are now at a point in your life where you had enough of your own toxicity and want to heal.

Are you ready to slowly take a step into the right direction? Well, let's go! Chapter 1 will kick off by explaining the different types of narcissism and help you identify with one in order to recognize which parts of yourself need the most attention and healing.

1

THE

NARCISSISTIC SPECTRUM

Narcissism is a trending topic that most people talk about; they even label others as narcissists but few know what it means to be a narcissist. Colleagues or team leaders who are controlling may place strain on their workers, in which the workers label them as narcissistic. However, the workers sometimes fail to see how they are projecting their own narcissistic tendencies onto others. The truth is, we all have the ability to be narcissistic. This means we are all somewhere on the narcissistic spectrum, and to a certain extent, it has a healthy affect on our mental health: For example, we all need to be self-centered for a healthy amount of confidence and self-belief to exist. The problem occurs when the narcissistic personality trait is taken to extremes in which it could be labeled pathological. Therefore, it is important to recognize whether you have narcissistic personality disorder or simply identify with the narcissistic personality trait.

Narcissism is defined as extreme conceitedness in which it makes you disregard people's feelings around you, as well as have an inability to see how your behavior impacts others. At first glance, maybe even a few weeks or months after meeting someone, you are charming and charismatic toward them. Your narcissistic tendencies will not immediately surface in the beginning stages of relationships. However, you do tend to go for people who feed your ego and build relationships with individuals who reinforce your behaviors.

In this chapter, you will learn different types of narcissism, and you will find out where on the spectrum you may place yourself—if it is a healthy or unhealthy personality trait, or whether you have developed narcissistic personality disorder. This part of the chapter might be difficult, as it requires you to be honest with yourself about what and who you are. Hurtful realizations may arise, but remember, healing isn't all sunshine and roses. Be realistic on your journey of healing, as you will experience pain, and be hard on yourself every now and then; tears will fall as you start putting in the work. As long as you do not get stuck on an emotion and allow it to make you give up on healing, these are all healthy signs. The last chunk of the chapter deals with the causes as well as wanting to enlighten you on your journey forward.

NARCISSISTIC PERSONALITY DISORDER IN ACTION

From Vaknin (2019):

Sam presents with anhedonia (failure to enjoy or find pleasure in anything) and dysphoria bordering on depression. He complains of inability to tolerate people's stupidity and selfishness in a variety of settings. He admits that as a result of his "intellectual superiority" he is not well placed to interact with others or even to understand them and what they are going through. He is a recluse and fears that he is being mocked and ridiculed behind his back as a misfit and a freak. Throughout the first session, he frequently compares himself to a machine, a computer, or a member of an alien and advanced race, and talks about himself in the third person singular.

Life, bemoans Sam, has dealt him a bad hand. He is consistently and repeatedly victimized by his clients, for instance. They take credit for his ideas and leverage them to promote themselves, but then fail to re-hire him as a consultant. He seems to attract hostility and animosity incommensurate with his good and generous deeds. He even describes being stalked by two or three vicious women whom he had spurned, he claims, not without pride in his own implied irresistibility. Yes, he is abrasive and contemptuous of others at times but only in the interests of "tough love." He is never obnoxious or gratuitously offensive.

Sam is convinced that people envy him and are "out to get him" (persecutory delusions). He feels that his work (he is also a writer) is not appreciated because of its elitist nature (high-brow vocabulary and such). He refuses to "dumb down". Instead, he is on a mission to educate his readers and clients and "bring them up to his level." When he describes his day, it becomes clear that he is desultory, indolent, and lacks self-discipline and regular working habits. He is fiercely independent and highly values his self-imputed "brutal honesty" and "original, non-herd, outside the box" thinking.

He is married but sexually inactive. Sex bores him and he regards it as a "low-level" activity practiced by "empty-headed" folk. He has better uses for his limited time. He is aware of his own mortality and conscious of his intellectual legacy. Hence his sense of entitlement. He never goes through established channels. Instead, he uses his connections to secure anything from medical care to car repair. He expects to be treated by the best but is reluctant to buy their services, holding himself to be their equal in his own field of activity. He gives little or no thought to the needs, wishes, fears, hopes, priorities, and choices of his nearest and dearest. He is startled and hurt when they become assertive and exercise their personal autonomy (for instance, by setting boundaries).

Sam is disarmingly self-aware and readily lists his weaknesses and faults - but only in order to preempt real scrutiny or to fish for compliments. He constantly brags about his achievements but feels deprived ("I deserve more, much more than that"). When any of his assertions or assumptions is challenged he condescendingly tries to prove his case. If he fails to convert his interlocutor, he sulks and even rages. He tends to idealize everyone or devalue them: people are either clever and good or stupid and malicious. But, everyone is a potential foe.

Sam is very hypervigilant and anxious. He expects the worst and feels vindicated and superior when he is punished ("martyred and victimized"). Sam rarely assumes total responsibility for his actions or accepts their consequences. He has an external locus of control and his defenses are alloplastic. In other words: he blames the world for his failures, defeats, and "bad luck". This "cosmic conspiracy" against him is why his grandiose projects keep flopping and why he is so frustrated.

VARIATIONS ON THE SPECTRUM

The most common label people are quick to use is "narcissist," forgetting or not knowing that there are different types of narcissism that exist and originate from different causes. Here we look at two main types of narcissism (grandiose and vulnerable narcissism), followed by narcissistic personality disorder. Brogaard (2019) states both subtypes of narcissism have self-centeredness as a core feature, but self-absorption is expressed differently in the two cases. Moreover, none of the three types of narcissism mentioned in this section can be viewed as better than the other because they all have their own problematic version of the same condition.

Grandiose Narcissism

If you fall under the category of grandiose narcissism, it means you hold yourself in high regard, brag often, feel entitled, show aggressive behavior, and are insensitive toward others. Your level of grandiosity is tested by analyzing your responses on a five point scale to the following statements:

- "I become obsessed with getting recognition for my achievements"
- "I frequently think about getting rewarded and seen for the efforts I make"
- "Everything I do, is for the world to be proud of me"

Grandiose narcissists believe they are special and should be treated as such. They may have an attitude that screams "I'm a know-it-all," as they are the type to always know better, even if information is provided by experts. One thing about a grandiose narcissist is that they believe they are never wrong. When we compare grandiose narcissists with people who have narcissistic personality disorder, we distinguish grandiose narcissists by their extroverted personality and some symptoms will be exaggerated. Grandiose narcissists only care about their own needs and disregards the needs of others. For example, within relationships they are only concerned with getting their needs met, but do not care if their partner or friend's needs are fulfilled. Relationships with a grandiose narcissist are one-sided, as they lack the ability to reciprocate what they require.

The following is a list of symptoms of people with grandiose narcissism (Patterson, 2021):

- You have a need to be admired by the people you engage with.
- You lack empathy for others.
- You have an exaggerated sense of importance in relationships and other areas of life.
- You have persistent fantasies of increased success, power, happiness, love, intelligence, or physical appearance.
- You believe that you are so special that you should only associate yourself with people who share similar qualities as yourself.
- You believe that you should receive special treatment and care wherever you go.
- You have a tendency to take advantage of other people or situations to fulfill your goals.
- You are envious of others and think others are envious of you.
- You come across as arrogant, conceited, or self-absorbed at all times.
- You have an extremely high self-esteem and level of confidence.
- You strongly believe that you are superior.

- You are impulsive and quick to react with anger, hostility, and verbal or physical aggression when confronted by others about your behavior.
- You take advantage of others.

Do you recognize some of the following signs of grandiose narcissism within yourself?

- You tend to be flashy and show off with expensive cars, clothes, and homes.
- You are always boastful and bragging about your accomplishments.
- You are inauthentic with compliments.
- You are quick to anger if anyone contradicts or disagrees with your beliefs or opinions.
- You stick to your views or opinions, even when there is plenty of evidence against them.

Vulnerable Narcissism

Vulnerable narcissism, also known as covert narcissism, refers to someone who has a low self-esteem, acts avoidant, and is hypersensitive and always on the lookout for criticism. They are fragile individuals who are unable to cope with the harshness of this world. This type of narcissism develops as a means of protection against feelings of not being good enough. However, they feel touched and disrespected when others do not give them special treatment. Vulnerable narcissism is tested by assessing your response on a five point scale to the following kind of statements:

- "I find it difficult to like myself unless someone else show that they like me"
- "I find it difficult to express what I feel inside"
- "I enjoy a friend circle who can depend on me because it makes me feel like I matter"

Even though they are such vulnerable and defensive beings, they still have a need for other people's validation to feed their ego. The avoidant behavior and passive attitude occurs as a result of feeling criticized or underestimated by their circle. According to Zajenkowski et al. (n.d.), people who show signs of vulnerable narcissism are associated with lower levels of self esteem, extraversion and agreeableness, higher neuroticism, a negative view of the past, and a fatalistic attitude.

Where grandiose narcissists would be flashy and boastful, vulnerable narcissists appear to be introverted, anxious, and experience symptoms of depression. Vulnerable narcissists have grandiose fantasies, but are timid and insecure, and consequently do not appear narcissistic on the surface (Wright & Furnham, 2014). Within some individuals, their behavior might mimic that of a mental illness: for example, bipolar disorder or a form of anxiety disorder. They tend to be rude and show anger at others, but only to hide their insecurities. Vulnerable narcissists will blame and deflect their vulnerabilities onto others while self-sabotaging and abandoning their boundaries to people please and feel accepted by the world.

Let's see if you can identify with some of the following signs of vulnerable narcissism (Dempsey, n.d.; Saxena, 2021):

- You have many friends, but your behavior and actions do not allow you to have close, personal, and intimate relationships.
- You have a need to be the center of attention, do things to be noticed, and don't reciprocate in relationships.
- You have the inability to see that you have hurt someone.
- Your main focus is yourself, to the extent that you do not care about others but you expect others to emotionally support you.
- Your friends are seasonal. The friendship only lasts for as long as it can benefit you.
- If someone doesn't feed your ego (for example, compliment you), it activates a feeling of shame within.
- You are fragile and triggered easily.
- You have a hard time dealing with failure and trauma.
- You overthink about how others perceive you.
- You are hard on yourself when you feel distressed or disappointed.
- You don't handle rejection well but end up agreeing with the person who rejected you as a way to reduce feeling shameful.
- You often experience a depressed mood.
- You tend to leave a social event if you feel it's not up to standard.
- You fear disappointment and are ashamed of needing others.
- You throw tantrums when things don't go your way and feel ashamed about it later.
- You tend to put the blame on other people.

- You feel jealous about things you believe you should have but don't have.

Narcissistic Personality Disorder

Barlow et al. (2017) defines narcissistic personality disorder as a disorder that involves a pervasive pattern of grandiosity in fantasy or behavior, need for admiration and lack of empathy. Narcissists tend to have the inability to self-regulate and to boost their self-esteem with an internal locus thus leading them to act out and seek attention from others to uplift their self-esteem. People with this disorder have a set of beliefs that they are the most important and should be treated as such. They tend to exaggerate their traits and abilities. For example, they might claim they are the most beautiful person in the building, or they are the smartest person in their department at work. Below you will find the diagnostic criteria for narcissistic personality disorder (Barlow et al., 2017).

A pervasive pattern of grandiosity (in fantasy or behavior), need for admiration and lack of empathy, beginning by early adulthood and present in a variety of contexts, as indicated by five or more of the following:

1. Has a grandiose sense of self-importance: for example, exaggerates achievements and talents and expects to be recognized as superior without matching achievements.
2. Is preoccupied with fantasies of unlimited success, power, brilliance, beauty or ideal love.

3. Believes that he or she is special and unique and can only be understood by, or should associate with, other special or high status people or institutions.
4. Requests excessive admiration.
5. Has a sense of entitlement for example, unreasonable or automatic compliance with his or her expectations.
6. Is interpersonally exploitative for example, takes advantage of others to achieve his or her own ends
7. Lacks empathy such as being unwilling to recognize or identify with the feelings and needs of others.
8. Is often envious of others or believes others are envious of them.
9. Shows arrogant, haughty behaviors or attitudes.

Personality disorders can only be diagnosed over the age of 18, as it is believed when one turns 18 the personality becomes fixed or more stable. However, our personalities are ever changing and continuously developing as we experience life. Meaning if you are 22 years old, for example, other factors can still influence you to worsen some narcissistic traits which can eventually develop into narcissistic personality disorder.

CONTRAST BETWEEN NARCISSISM AND NARCISISSTIC PERSONALITY DISORDER

As said before, a certain degree of narcissism is healthy, but when you notice it affecting yourself and others around you negatively, that is when you need to recognize the need for concern. Healthy narcissism refers to someone who looks in the mirror and says "Oooh, I'm looking good today!" and admires themselves, which is good to keep your self-esteem from dropping; but it becomes a problem when you think your looks and beauty are a reason to be superior in every context of your life. Healthy narcissism refers to people who are secure in their bodies, have self-confidence and know their strengths and weaknesses. Also, they know their limits and when their behavior becomes too extra for the context they find themselves in.

Some people have narcissistic tendencies, but it does not mean they have a disorder. You may be such a competitive person at work and have a main aim of being promoted that you become selfish and will do anything to get the top spot no matter who gets hurt in the process. This is an example of being narcissistic, but it is not a personality disorder. People with narcissistic tendencies may still have the ability to empathize and be aware of what their behavior does to others by being regretful or questioning their actions. It becomes a disorder when your personality is centered around your narcissistic tendencies. Your thoughts and behavior become maladaptive, in which the trait, narcissism, is one of your main and most dominant personality traits. Furthermore, your mental health, work life, and relationships start to suffer as a result of your behavior.

Let's look at how narcissistic traits differs from narcissistic personality disorder:

- How often you engage in narcissistic behavior and the level of intensity thereof

We can categorize healthy narcissism, narcissistic traits, and narcissistic personality disorder by looking at how often someone shows narcissistic behavior, their intensity of the behavior and the impact it has on the relationships in one's life. In addition, another factor that tells us which category someone's behavior belongs to is whether the person is insightful and aware of how their behavior influences others. Someone with narcissistic personality disorder shows narcissistic behavior continuously, every day and in every situation, while someone who has the narcissistic trait will engage in narcissistic behavior frequently and only in certain situations. Also, people with narcissistic personality disorder are unable to celebrate when others are winning and lack awareness when their behavior hurts someone.

- You occasionally engage in self-centered behavior

Some days we may obsess over how good we look in a particular outfit, want to share our accomplishments on social media for attention from others, or even lash out and say regretful things to a loved one, but the behavior is not persistent. It is seen as normal if these behaviors happen occasionally. However, with a person who suffers from narcissistic personality disorder, the previously mentioned behaviors are persistent. For example, they want to be the center of attention all the time and when they are not, they start feeling depressed and distressed.

- You are able to be accountable and apologize when you are wrong

A healthy and normal level of narcissism refers to being able to apologize when you did someone wrong because you have empathy and see why the person may feel hurt by your actions. You will be able to reflect on your actions and return to the person with a sincere apology, but people with narcissistic personality disorder try to gaslight and act dramatic when someone tells them they are wrong. Someone with narcissistic personality disorder may respond to someone telling them "You are wrong and what you have said deeply hurt me" with, "No, you are just being sensitive, I didn't say anything wrong, it is not that deep." This causes damage to relationships as conflict is never resolved when the person with narcissistic personality disorder causes the problem. When a narcissist starts to feel threatened that their partner will leave, only then will they start to smother their partner with love and affection.

- Your reaction to cheating is reasonable and humane

Cheating on a partner who you claim to love shows narcissistic tendencies. It is how you respond to cheating that determines whether it is a normal level of narcissism or narcissistic personality disorder. Someone without narcissistic personality disorder will show guilt or regret and change their behavior as an attempt to rectify the situation, but someone with narcissistic personality disorder will love bomb their partner until they are forgiven and still continue cheating. No changed behavior will follow the apology because they are self-centered and only care about making themselves happy.

UNDERLYING CAUSES OF NPD

Narcissistic personality disorder can develop from a range of causes, such as:

Temperament

Our temperament characterizes our animal instincts. This is a driving force behind how we act; therefore, we say it's the behaviors we enact without learning it from our environment. Our temperament consists of stable, consistent behaviors that we are born with and most likely won't change as it is seen as permanent. If you were born with an oversensitive temperament, it can be a contributing factor to activate narcissistic personality disorder in your twenties. The influence of your temperament can be understood in two ways. The first one has an impact on the caregiver of the child. If the child is a difficult baby, a specific parenting style will be used to parent the child. Difficult and very sensitive babies usually have stressed out parents as a result of the child's temperament. An exhausted parent will lack the ability to thoroughly cater to the child's needs. For example, if a child is overly sensitive and cries easily, the parent might become angry at the child often, as it is embarrassing to go out in public with a child who cries for everything. Or, the parent could be the type to soften up when the child cries and gives them exactly what they are crying for. None of these reactions by the parent are healthy for the development of the child. The child will either retreat and become insecure due to the parent being angry when they want their needs met, or the child can become manipulative when they learn that every time they behave in a certain way the parent gives them their way, which puts the child at risk for vulnerable or grandiose narcissistic tendencies.

The second impact temperament may have is the type of temperament the child was born with puts them at risk for certain emotional, behavioral and cognitive stressors. This explains that both genetics and environmental factors combined play a role in the development of narcissistic personality disorder, as Wright & Furnham (2014) state that our personality traits are approximately 50% determined by our genetics.

Environmental factors

Environmental factors refer to your personality and how your parents raised you, as well as trauma that you experienced during childhood. Our personality consists of three components: the id, ego and superego. The id is responsible for our primary needs, the ego governs the realistic principles and makes a decision whether the id can get what he wants or not, and the superego refers to your conscience—knowing what is right and wrong. Think of a baby and how demanding they are. Any inconvenience they experience, they start crying, right? This occurs because their id is not satisfied. While this is okay for a baby to do, as an adult, the behavior may be seen as absurd. Babies or toddlers may be described as self-centered and grandiose as a result of not having a fully developed personality yet.

However, if the child was not guided by parents and taught empathy and altruism from a young age, they tend to stay fixed in a stage where their needs are always met, and life revolves around them only. As the child develops into an adult, they will keep seeking and chasing someone who will meet their needs, but will never find what they truly need. It is believed that parents or family members who excessively pampered or treated you as superior may be linked to the development of narcissistic personality disorder. This refers to parents who would shower you with praise, treat you like royalty and admire you every chance they get. As a result of this, you feel people from your external environment should match the behavior toward you of the people in your internal environment. This becomes the child who later develops into an adult who presents grandiose narcissistic tendencies. According to WebMD Editorial Contributors (2020), people who present with covert or vulnerable narcissistic traits were abused or neglected as a child. This is the child who grew up in an environment where parents do not meet their physical and emotional needs: for example, growing up with low socioeconomic status.

Parenting style also plays a role in the development of narcissistic personality disorder. Strict and overprotective parents who act as helicopters make children feel inferior and small. These parents also have unrealistic expectations from their children, or they excessively praise good behaviors and excessively criticize bad behaviors. Yes, parents are supposed to be the superior one in the parent-child relationship, but they should give the child their freedom to make decisions on their own as this could either cause the child to become insecure or to mimic their behavior as an adult. As an adult, this child may have difficulty making decisions and expect others to be authoritative. They become individuals with low-esteem, extremely fragile and hypersensitive to criticism. Pedersen (2021) states that research suggests that overprotective parenting was linked to both vulnerable and grandiose narcissism in young adults.

More parental factors that are linked to the development of narcissistic personality disorder:

- growing up with a parent who suffered from a mental illness
- learning manipulative behavior from parents or peers
- inconsistent or unpredictable parental caregiving
- parents being too lenient
- lack of love and affection in parent-child relationships

The last environmental factor we will look at is socio-cultural factors. Research claims that narcissism scores were higher in individualistic cultures (which focus more on each person's rights and goals) compared with collectivistic cultures (which focus more on what's best for the group) (Pedersen, 2021). Narcissistic personality disorder is on the rise especially in western societies where individualism is promoted. People are taught to be competitive, to only care about themselves, throw collectivism in the bin and have a mindset that says, "each to their own." Individualism may create more introverted people who are self-focused. Most people in today's society are hyper focused on moving forward, reaching their goals, being independent and bettering themselves. They are also the type to post on social media and seek validation from strangers to feed the ego. Moreover, on social media lots of memes and online communities promote the idea of self-love: for example, this quote found on Facebook states "Normalize being obsessed with yourself and not caring what anyone else thinks", which could be a reason why most people become so self-absorbed. In addition, Barlow et al. (2017) claims that the spike in research on narcissism may also be a contributing factor as to why the prevalence of narcissistic personality disorder is on the rise. The culture of individualism, entitlement and materialistic values are the main elements of narcissism.

Neurobiological

One of the marked characteristics of pathological narcissism is having a lack of empathy and research shows that the amount of empathy is directly correlated to the volume of gray brain matter of the corresponding cortical representation in the insular region, and that the patients with narcissism exhibit a structural deficit in exactly this area (*Altered Brain Structure in Pathological Narcissism,* 2013). Also, we learn from Bartosch (2020) that narcissistic personality disorder is marked by increased oxidative stress in the blood and is also connected to interpersonal hypersensitivity.

THE CASE FOR CHANGING BEHAVIORAL PATTERNS

There is no cure for narcissistic tendencies or narcissistic personality disorder. Remember, narcissism is a personality trait that cannot be removed; we can only decide to use it in a healthier manner. You may have been sold the idea that narcissism can be cured, but it is not true. Mental health issues cannot be cured overnight, they can only be treated on a regular basis. Treatment won't run smoothly; you will have off days and there will be days where you can celebrate your progress. There is no cure for narcissistic personality disorder or having the narcissistic trait. However, if you believe with every fiber in your body that you can change, you will change. Change will only occur if you strongly believe in yourself, in great need or dying to change.

The type of treatment recommended by a therapist is based on the severity of your narcissistic tendencies as well as the symptoms you are experiencing. Psychodynamic, behavioral, and cognitive therapies are popular for treating narcissism. In addition, another therapy that is used refers to metacognitive interpersonal therapy. Psychodynamic therapy will attempt to give you more insight on your problem, for instance make you aware of where it is coming from, childhood, abuse, trauma, parent-child relationships and so forth. Behavioral therapy will help you to see how your behavior negatively impacts yourself and relationships while cognitive therapy helps to improve developmental issues as well as reframe some distorted thoughts and beliefs that may exist in you by using various strategies. These strategies will replace unhealthy behaviors and beliefs with healthier ones that will benefit your well-being and relationships. The main aim of metacognitive interpersonal therapy is to help you see your unrealistic standards, to change them and to be content with your own level of productivity.

When you commit to therapy, there are some steps that need to be followed. Here are five essential steps (Raypole, 2020):

1. Identifying existing defense mechanisms

2. Exploring reasons behind these coping methods

3. Learning and practicing new patterns of behavior

4. Exploring how behaviors affect others

5. Examining connections between your internal voice
   and how you treat others

In the chapters that follow, we look at five ways to improve your narcissistic tendencies through:

- *Mindfulness*—mindfulness is a technique that will teach you how to be present and to accept the moment for what it is, which will allow inferior complexes and expectations of others to subside as well as working with your narcissistic urges.

- *Focusing on gratitude*—this will teach you to be grateful and to reciprocate the energy of another person.

- *Going outwards instead of inwards*—chapter four encourages you to practice self-compassion instead of self-promotion.

- *Cognitive behavioral therapy*—this is a technique widely used by therapists to transform thoughts and behaviors that negatively impact the self.

- *Reparenting the inner child*—this strategy helps you uncover traumas and gives you an opportunity to reparent yourself so that the inner child is happy and allows the adult version of yourself to flourish.

2

THE TRANSITION TO MINDFULNESS

In the previous chapter, you were able to place yourself into a category of healthy narcissism, toxic narcissism, and narcissistic personality disorder. If you made it thus far, you probably identified toxic narcissistic tendencies in yourself or self-diagnosed with narcissistic personality disorder. It is essential that you know exactly what category you fall into, without lying to yourself and sugarcoating how bad your narcissistic tendencies actually affect the self and others, as this will help you to correctly use the techniques provided in this chapter.

The first step to improving your narcissism is making you aware and helping you gain insight on your personality problem through engaging in mindfulness practices. Not only will it help you to identify in which situations you are mostly narcissistic, but it will help you to obtain a state where you will realize you are enough and don't need outside factors to validate your existence or believe that the world owes you something. You do not need any tools to be mindful because each and every human already possesses the ability to be mindful. However, here are a list of things you will need for your first step toward healing:

- Time from your busy, fast paced life
- An attitude that aligns with healing and mindfulness
- A willingness to be mindful
- the ability to sit with uncomfortable feelings and Thoughts that will arise
- The ability to love yourself and to be kind toward yourself when you come to hurtful realizations

In this chapter, you will learn what it is to be mindful and how it is linked to improving narcissistic traits. There is a lack of research that covers mindfulness and narcissism in which most articles state that mindfulness practices may promote the development of narcissism. However, here you will learn how to use the mindfulness technique in a way that will benefit you and not push you deeper down a path of destruction. Lastly, you will be provided with some mindfulness techniques as well as the benefits that come with mindfulness practices.

Allow this chapter to make you become more mindful of your actions, in order to build a better you!

UNDERSTANDING MINDFULNESS

Mindfulness has become quite trendy in the modern world. Whether it is on social media, television, the radio, or word-of-mouth, you have heard or seen mindfulness being advertised widely. Mindfulness can be defined as becoming aware of something by solely focusing your attention on one specific thing with the main goal of being present in the moment without reacting to the thoughts that flow through the mind. During a mindfulness session, your mind takes flight and loses touch with your body which could make you feel anxious at first because it is not your usual way of knowing reality. To be mindful means to experience the present moment by allowing yourself to be fully in control without being overwhelmed by any external or internal factors.

Mindfulness can be practiced in various settings and in many different ways. For the sake of this book, you will be taught how to practice mindfulness as an attempt to recognize your own narcissistic traits. For many narcissists, their behavior is not a problem, and they are unable to identify when they are hurting another person emotionally. Thus, mindfulness will create a platform where you can be still, analyze your behavior and become more aware of who you are and how you operate in the world. Yes, you might be told by someone, "You are self-centered and insensitive!" but are you able to see it for yourself? Not always. Narcissists tend to lash out with aggressiveness when they are confronted and accused of their negative behaviors. Therefore, when you become mindful of your own behaviors it is easier for you to understand why others feel a certain way toward you and why your relationships never seem to work or go as well as you expect it to develop.

Same as habits, narcissistic traits are strengthened through continuously wanting to satisfy the ego. You will find a trigger, have a behavior that follows being triggered and then get a reward from that behavior which is an ego boost in a narcissist's case. From a young age, parents or others in your environment might have pampered you and made you feel like the most important person in their worlds, in which as an adult out of habit, you expect others to also feed your ego like your loved ones did. This is all you know, this is how you believe people should treat you. Mindfulness can act as a tool that will access parts of you that will allow those unrealistic beliefs and expectations to tear apart, and to start on a clean page with new beliefs to live from. It will help you to observe and to understand the mechanics behind your narcissistic behaviors. As you journey through life as a narcissist, you may never have thought that your natural way of doing things could be destroying your mental health and your relationships with others. We all have habits that we do not notice that we engage in, but others are able to. Mindfulness will be the friend that switches on the light, allows you to see your bad habits and break the habit mode you find yourself in by primarily making use of narcissistic traits to navigate through life.

IMPROVING NARCISSISTIC TENDENCIES

According to Passfield (2019), mindfulness meditation can assist you in reducing narcissistic traits and help you to cope with the damages done to relationships. Many of us live life with norms, habits and beliefs that we have been stuck on since childhood not knowing that as an adult, what we have been taught becomes outdated. Some rules and beliefs only apply to certain developmental stages of our life, and once we outgrow them, the rules and beliefs change. However, as a narcissist, you did not unlearn any childhood rules and beliefs thus creating high expectations of others within personal and work relationships.

You may wonder, *How will breathing and focusing on observing your thoughts and behavior, miraculously improve your ways?* Well, here are ways how mindfulness improves your narcissistic tendencies:

- Mindfulness challenges the stories you tell about yourself and the world around you.

Narcissists are fragile and vulnerable beings that often experience negative feelings as a result of negative self-stories. The stories that you tell yourself and believe about yourself are deflected upon the people you work with or are in relationships with. For example, you may criticize a colleague by attacking their self-esteem and breaking down their self-worth, sometimes in front of others. By frequently practicing mindfulness, you will learn where your narcissistic ways stem from as well as find a balanced and less distorted view of your self-worth.

- Creates a stepping stone for the creation of healthy self-confidence.

Narcissists come across as people with inflated self-confidence in which they start treating others that they believe are beneath them poorly or do not associate themselves with them at all. Because of the high self-confidence, you feel superior and expect people to treat you with special care and attention. Mindfulness will alter deficit thinking and the need for attention from others therefore attention-seeking behaviors will eventually become distinct. In order to gain an optimal and healthy level of self-confidence, it is recommended that you become mindful of the positive and humbling experiences you encounter. When you place your focus on a positive occurrence, you need to be able to allow the mind and body to fully engage in the thoughts without having a need from an external force to validate it. Passfiel (2019) states that by enriching the positive experience by absorbing with your brain and body, you change your neural pathways. In other words, you rewire your brain for better and healthier connections. In this way, you become humble and content with who you are. Being self-sufficient is also a by-product of this exercise as you start to believe you are enough and do not need approval of others to feed the ego.

- Transforms the belief that you are better and more superior than others.

Narcissists possess a built in superiority complex and their behavior is driven by a need to keep this belief on a pedestal. The things you do are either to gain or to demonstrate your superiority over others. At work, you may act like the boss even though that is not your job description, or you have a need to always be the dominant person in all your relationships. Another example refers to if someone sent you a picture of their plant and said, "It's growing and becoming so pretty," you would reply with "I'm prettier than the plant." Everything always has to be about you. You believe you are better than the next person, smarter and more inclined to make decisions that they cannot make. This is the attitude that pushes people away, because most of the time their suggestions and opinions do not count in your eyes. You would rather choose your way of doing things than to listen and use the opinion of another person. Mindfulness meditation practices will act as your support system when you say to yourself, *I don't have a need to be superior in all areas of my life; I should only do what my job description says/I only need to play the role that I was assigned to*. When you do a mindfulness practice, you are teaching yourself to be kind and loving which will enrich and heal a fragile ego. In addition, when you learn to be kind and loving toward yourself, you will be able to show compassion and appreciation for other peoples' happiness and achievements without being envious.

- Mindfulness will increase your level of self-awareness.

Narcissists often have a low level of self-awareness. You may be unaware of where your narcissistic traits stem from or even that you are narcissistic. Many may label you as a narcissist, but you will brush it off or become angry about it. Once you are able to gain insight on your true self and how your personality has become the villain in many people's lives, you can start working on improving narcissistic tendencies. Mindfulness practice is a method that you can use to deepen self-knowledge in order to become more self-aware. This may be difficult and the knowledge you will learn about yourself will be uncomfortable to process.   Mindfulness will shed light on the parts of yourself that you want to avoid or rather choose not to know about. It is a way to educate yourself about yourself as your behaviors have been kept in the dark by your brain. Moreover, mindfulness will wake you up to the reality of who you truly are. It will educate you on your triggers, how you habitually respond, and teach you a way to manage your narcissistic tendencies to mitigate harm done to your internal environment and to those around you.

- Recognizing "people pleasing" tendencies.

Narcissists are charming and want to please others so that these people can feed their ego with compliments and shower them with appreciation. You also engage in people pleasing tendencies as an attempt to not be criticized by them, because being criticized riles you up. You will go to the ends of the earth even if it means self-sabotaging and disrespecting your own boundaries to please others, which is unhealthy and only feeds a perpetual cycle of insecurity and a fragile ego. Through mindfulness, you can develop a stronger love for yourself. You can reset boundaries and promise yourself to stick to it. At first, your ego will suffer, you will feel hurt and distressed; but remember, it has to rain before you can see a rainbow. Mindfulness will allow you to love yourself deeply and to self-regulate without the help of others.

- Mindfulness meditation can help you ease the trauma of growing up with a narcissistic parent.

It is common to become a narcissist in your adult life if you have a narcissistic parent. They modeled this behavior and you have soaked it up. Parents are our first teachers; we learn from them how to be a person. How a parent treats a child is how the child will treat others. It is known that a narcissistic person usually engages in three key strategies that will have lifelong effects on their victims: Idealize, devalue, and discard. Engaging in mindfulness meditation will rewire the brain, and allow you to become self-compassionate which will disconnect you from old beliefs and values that were ingrained into your identity from a young age.

PUTTING IT INTO ACTION

Just like there are many reasons to use mindfulness, there are also various ways to bring the mind to a mindfulness state. Below will be discussed three popular mindfulness meditations (Mayo Clinic Staff, 2020):

- **Body scan meditation:** A body scan is done by lying on your back with your arms resting beside you. The next thing you have to do is place your full attention on every body part, from toes to the head.

- **Sitting meditation:** Sit in a comfortable position and ensure that your back is straight, not hunched. Allow your feet to be flat on the floor while placing your hands in your lap. Now you need to bring your mind to a calm state and breathe. Inhale through the nose, and exhale through the mouth with lips pursed.

- **Walking meditation:** Find a time and a safe place to go for a mindful walk. Take a slow walk and be fully engaged in the experience.

There are more ways to be mindful but all of them have the same principles. For all the above mentioned meditations, you also need to become aware of sensations, thoughts and emotions that arise during your meditative state. However, it is recommended not to get lost in those sensations, emotions or thoughts. Trauma is deeply stored in the body therefore when doing a body scan, you need to pay attention to which parts of the body feels painful or uncomfortable, and what kind of thoughts pop up once you think of your leg for example. Also, thinking of certain body parts may take you back to an event in your life that caused trauma. The same rule applies for walking and sitting meditations.

As stated previously, narcissistic tendencies can be seen in the same light as bad habits we possess as humans. This means it can be treated in the same manner when it comes to using mindfulness to create awareness around your narcissistic traits. Here are four steps to follow to attempt breaking narcissistic habits through meditation:

1. **Identify and become more aware of the narcissistic tendency you want to change**

Think about which actions you can take to avoid acting out in a narcissistic manner. What is an alternative or healthier reaction you can use? For example, every time your partner confronts you, you get angry and give them the silent treatment for days. A healthier choice would be to listen carefully to your partner, and show them that you are trying to understand where they are coming from. Communicate instead of ignoring your partner.

2. Work with the trigger that urges you to become narcissistic

Make a note of what triggers you. Identify the people, environment, time of day, and sensations you experience when feeling triggered. Does it occur in public or behind closed doors? Every detail of your trigger should be taken into account. Once you become aware of your triggers, you can stop the habitual behavior of being narcissistic. Remember, our brains are lazy and take mental shortcuts which means it will respond in ways that the brain has been wired for. Now that you know your behavior and wiring of the brain is toxic and sabotaging, you need to actively step in and change it. In order to be in control of the brain so that it does not respond habitually, mindfulness will be your best friend. When you feel the urge to be narcissistic, allow yourself to take a step back and breathe. Pausing before reacting will reprogram the brain to respond differently. Also, notice your internal state. Which feeling is most dominant? For example, feelings of anxiety, discomfort, bodily sensations, distressed or a combination of distorted thoughts and feelings.

3. Fully engage in the experience instead of acting on the trigger

Be willing to sit with the feelings or thoughts that are most dominant. Note that this will be difficult, but you will have to fight your urge to be narcissistic. You may feel the need to mention your achievements when your friend tells you they are graduating next month. Instead of making the conversation about yourself, take a deep breath to release the feelings associated with the urge and show that you are proud of your friend and are happy for them. However, you do not have to respond with a healthier reaction. As a newbie on your healing path, take it slow and know that it is enough to pause and smile even if it does not feel genuine.

4. **Allow yourself to be okay with whatever feeling arises**

During this step, the brain will go into an anxious state as it is not used to functioning in this way. Sit with the feeling, and be kind toward yourself and the situation at hand while continuing to take deep breaths.

Now that you know how to work on breaking a habit of being narcissistic, let's look at the six steps to make mindfulness a habit and part of your daily routine. Becoming mindful of your breathing pattern is a great way to gain awareness on aspects you would usually ignore.

Practice the following six steps to form the habit of engaging in mindfulness frequently:

1. Find a comfortable and suitable space that you can regularly use as your mindfulness spot. The space you choose should have minimal to no disturbances for example, your bedroom. Also, make the spot you chose

feel and look like a meditation setting. Add a meditation pillow, a Buddha statue or hang a tapestry on the wall. Decorating the room is optional but once you invested money into making a special spot for meditation purposes, you will be more inclined to use it. Lastly, ensure that your space radiates peace and tranquility.

2. Find a time during your day that fits into your schedule and suits your temperament. If you are not a morning person, choose to do your mindfulness practice when you get home from work or if you are someone who is exhausted when you get from work, try doing it as soon as you wake up in the morning. Whatever time suits you best, use that time of your day as your mindfulness practice slot. Start your mindfulness meditations off with 10 to 15 minutes of practice. As you gradually make progress by mindfulness becoming a habit, you can start meditating for longer time periods for example, engaging in 20 to 25 minute sessions.

3. Position yourself on your meditation pillow in a comfortable manner that will allow you to sit up straight. Relax your body, sit firmly feeling your weight planted on the cushion with the floor beneath you, and close your eyes. Notice any tension in the body and allow it to be released before officially starting your meditation session. Then, let go of any worries that hinder the mind.

4. Breathe in your natural rhythm and focus your attention on the sensations you experience. Which of the five senses are dominant in that moment? You may feel a gentle and cool breeze through the nostrils as you breathe, and how the chest or stomach moves as you inhale and exhale.

5. Once breathing becomes natural, you may experience intrusive thoughts and emotions creeping up on you. Do not beat yourself up for losing focus, kindly allow yourself to get back into the meditative state with your breath as a guide. Note where your mind wandered to for instance, your nose started itching, or your thoughts got stuck on something that happened during your day or the day before.

6. Do not force a perfect breathing pattern. Allow your breathing to flow naturally whether it is slow, rough or long. When breathing becomes slower, let it calm your internal environment.

Once mindfulness meditation becomes embedded into your daily routine, you will start to use it without having to remind yourself. It will become habitual such as showering or brushing teeth everyday.

WHAT TO ACTUALLY GAIN FROM IT

Although the benefits will be in the back of your mind when you think about mindfulness, it is recommended that you do not fixate on it nor is it healthy to have expectations of rapid changes after engaging in a few sessions. Mindfulness has many benefits such as reducing stress, enhancing well-being, increasing productivity and so forth but in this section, we will only focus on how it will benefit you as a narcissist with a goal of improving into a healthier version of yourself.

Let's unpack eight benefits of mindfulness practices for narcissists:

- Mindfulness stimulates happy hormones in the brain. Overall it has a positive influence on the mind. Research states that mindfulness can act as an antidepressant (*Why Practice It?*, n.d.). Depressive moods are often experienced by narcissists as they often feel alone, aggressive and fragile—their egos can be bruised easily. In addition, knowing how to manipulate the brain into providing it with happy hormones will make you less dependent on others to boost your self-esteem.

- Mindfulness rewires and reprograms the brain for healthier pathways to be cultivated. Studies have shown that mindfulness can generate the parts of the brain that controls emotional regulation and empathy. These are both factors that narcissists often score low on because they cannot regulate their own emotions without picking on others or having others feed their egos. Empathy is a trait that most narcissistic individuals need to improve on. You will need this to create long lasting relationships with others. Without empathy, you are unable to understand the people around you.

- Mindfulness improves our humanitarianism. Regular mindfulness sessions will lead to being compassionate toward ourselves and others. This could benefit you in creating stronger and closer connections with others as you will learn to help others even if it doesn't benefit you in any way.

- Mindfulness helps you to create a better and more improved version of yourself which will overflow into your personal and work relationships. This will make you a calmer, less reactive and more optimistic individual in your relationships. Moreover, in romantic relationships it is believed that couples will handle conflict in a healthier manner and bounce back from quarrels quickly.

- Mindfulness changes our perspective of ourselves. People who engage in meditation have a stronger sense of self-worth, stick to their values and do not allow others to overstep their boundaries. *Why Practice It?* (n.d.) states mindfulness may increase feelings of being secure within your own body and having the ability to deal with criticism.

- Mindfulness gives us the power to handle and to recover from bad situations easily. You are sensitive and dealing with negativity in a healthy way is not your forte. Mindfulness will come in handy when you are being confronted by others or made aware that you were wrong and caused damage to relationships. Bad situations you get yourself into won't be something that you get lost in and deflect onto others.

- As a narcissist, you tend to be biased when it comes to groups that differ from you. You choose to only mingle with the ones you believe are on your level. Mindfulness mitigates the tendency to be biased and judgmental.

- For the narcissists who have children, mindfulness practices benefit parents and caregivers. It allows the mental health of parents to be stable and in check so that you can raise your children without projecting your inner turmoil and past traumas onto children. Also, healthier parents fosters healthier children which boosts their development. Parents who are not anxious, depressed or stressed are able to pay more attention to their children. If you are a parent, mindfulness will aid you in enhancing your well-being and bring awareness to your toxic traits in order to be a better parent to your child.

3

PRACTICING GRATITUDE HABITUALLY

The first step encourages you to become mindful, identify and manage your triggers, and to be okay with the present moment. The second step involves learning how to be grateful. Your narcissistic personality blinds you from being appreciative of others and the little things that light up life. It builds a wall that leaves you on the darker side of life, unable to experience the brighter side of the world. You may think, *Why should I be thankful if someone compliments me?* because you believe you are entitled to be complimented by others—it is how it "must" be. This applies to when others offer to help you or when you are blessed by an unseen force as well. Growing up, you might have been praised and admired for your good looks or people extend their help without you asking. As an adult you feel this is how the world is supposed to treat you. For the vulnerable narcissist, the opposite occurred while growing up. Parents and others may have criticized your appearance and left you to be independent. Being independent from a young age, with minimal to no help or support from a trusted adult can be seen as neglect. Because you have not received a certain treatment during childhood, you may believe the world owes it to you as an adult as well as needing others to validate you.

In this chapter, we motivate you to unlearn your expectations of the world by teaching you to be grateful whenever someone compliments you, helps you in any way or puts a smile on your face. We will only focus on helping you to become more grateful toward the people in your life as the main goal of this book is to improve your personality in order to mend broken relationships and to maintain ones that are still in good condition. Topics that will be discussed within this chapter refers to defining gratitude, how narcissism becomes a thieve of thankfulness, and teaching you how to practice gratitude. Lastly, we look at how practicing gratitude can improve your narcissistic tendencies.

For step two in the process of improving your narcissistic personality, you must be willing to act in a way that is out of your comfort zone and that deviates from your existing beliefs.

UNDERSTANDING GRATITUDE

Neurotypicals were taught from a young age to say "please and thank you" when someone has been kind to them: for example, receiving a gift from an aunt or being told "You look beautiful/handsome today." This behavior then becomes an automatic response as they grow older. They are taught by caregivers that it is a social rule that needs to be followed as a way to be polite, respectful and considerate toward another person. In your case, parents and caregivers may have spoiled you as a child or you were isolated from the world as you grew up with strict and authoritative parents. This means you either got everything you wanted, or you never had the opportunity to learn the social rule of expressing your appreciation for another person. However, you are able to accept gratitude expressions from others, but you are unable to reciprocate the act.

Mayor Galindo (2021) defines gratitude as a conscious, positive emotion one can express when feeling thankful for something, whether tangible or intangible. Expressing gratitude is more than following the rules of society. It is a way to acknowledge another individual's kindness toward you as well as having the ability to see when life is treating you well. Gratitude can be categorized as (Cherry, 2021):

- a personality trait. Have you noticed that some people are just naturally more grateful than others? This is a direct reflection of their personality and the person's general disposition.

- a mood. This means that a person may not experience being grateful all the time but only certain time periods.

- an emotion. Gratitude is seen as an emotion when an individual only experiences being grateful in the moment.

Gratitude is not something that has been ingrained into your personality nor has it been modeled in front of you which makes it hard to see why gratitude is important or should be expressed.

ACKNOWLEDGEMENT AND NARCISSISTIC TENDENCIES

With the wide range of personality traits, it is believed that narcissists do not have the capacity to be grateful for anything. Egocentrism, cynicism, materialism, and narcissism are known to be the thieves that take away your ability to thank others and to recognize when they are expressing kind gestures toward you. You refuse to acknowledge that someone has freely without reason, blessed you with kind words, loving actions or physical gifts. Your inflated self-esteem and self-centeredness leads to forgetting that people do not owe you or have an obligation to feed your ego, help you or to buy you a gift on your birthday. You feel entitled to receiving the love and kindness from others and therefore think you have no reason to thank them. In your mind you may think, *I deserve this!* but the hard truth is, the world or people doesn't owe you anything. Both the grandiose and vulnerable narcissist will have this attitude toward life. The traits that you possess which are most dominant in your personality skews your perspective of gratitude. Your beliefs of the world also play a large role in why you do not express gratitude. If you keep expecting someone to do something, you will not be thankful for it. Empathy is not one of the traits that you score well in thus making it hard to understand or match the efforts of another. Most narcissists support individualistic views and believe that everyone acts out of self-interest as this is how you operate in life. You move through life by only doing things that will benefit you, no matter if it is harmful to the other person.

Let's look at two studies that focused on gratitude and narcissistic tendencies (Allen, n.d.):

The first study done by Lisa Farwell and Ruth Wohlwend-Lloyd that attempts to demonstrate the relationship between gratitude and narcissism. In the study, people who participated were told two things: Their test results were compared with someone unknown to them and that they had done 85% better than them. People who are narcissistic reported feeling less grateful toward their partners in comparison with individuals who are less narcissistic. Narcissistic personality traits are believed to be a cause of people's decline in expressing gratitude.

The second study done in 2017 by Rebecca Solom, Phil Watkins, and colleagues tested undergraduate students who identify as narcissists as well as personality traits such as cynicism, materialism and envy. It was found that these students were less grateful being two months into the study even after controlling their gratitude levels at the beginning. According to Allen (n.d.), one reason for the negative association between narcissism and gratitude refers to a narcissist's sense of entitlement.

How to Evaluate Your Ability to Experience Gratitude

Answer the following questions with honesty in order to measure whether you are able to be grateful:

- Can you think of various things in your life to be grateful for?
- Will a list of things you feel thankful for be long?
- Do you think your ability to be grateful for both the little and big things in life has increased as you aged?
- Do you often appreciate random moments such as the sunset or a special person in your life?
- Do you have the ability to appreciate and be thankful for people who differ from you?

If you answered no to most of the above questions, don't fret! The following section of the chapter provides you with steps on making gratitude a habit and saying thank you with a sincere and authentic approach.

HABITUALLY MAKING GRATITUDE A PART OF YOUR SELF IMAGE

In order to develop and strengthen your capacity to be grateful, below we have divided gratitude into two stages.

Stage one: Identify how blessed you are even in dark times.

Whether things are going great, everything is happening in your favor or whether it feels like you are going downhill, there is always something to be grateful for. However, when life starts pushing us into a corner, we panic and our brain responds out of survival. The brain wants to protect you from danger in which it won't always act in your greatest interest. When you feel things are getting bad, there is a dark cloud hovering over your head, start counting your blessings. Focus on the things that are working out for you instead of hyper focusing on things that are going wrong. For example, when a relationship is not working out for you and you start feeling lonely, distract the brain from the unwanted feeling by thinking of something you are most grateful for in your life. Make sure you name something that does not add to your narcissism (for instance "I am grateful for the great body that I have" or "I am grateful that I am rich and have the ability to buy anything I desire"). It is recommended that you mention things that are not directly about you, such as "I am grateful to have a job, a roof over my head, and good health," "I am grateful to have people in my life who stick by my side no matter what," or "I am grateful to live another day."

Try to visualize all the things you are grateful for, once a day. Mayor Galindo (2021) supports this idea by stating when you do this practice everyday, you will start to identify the good things and experience a natural feeling of joy and gratitude. In addition, you will begin to accept and appreciate the little things that make life easier to deal with.

Stage two: Acknowledging that the source of your blessings are controlled by external factors and not yourself.

By recognizing how blessed you are in the present moment, you can easily do stage two. Stage two requires you to understand that all blessings and the goodness in your life comes from an external source. For you, this step to cultivating a capacity to be grateful might be hard as you need to let go of the idea that what you have accomplished thus far, is not only because of your own efforts but by the help of others and a force bigger than us. If you can accept this and believe it, you will naturally gravitate toward a more joyful and grateful self by being thankful for others and the Almighty. Gratitude gives us the ability to acknowledge and appreciate the connection we have with those around us for example, colleagues, neighbors, friends, family, sometimes even the random guy who decides to have a deep conversation with you in the grocery store. You will start to see how each one has a purpose in your life and contribute to who you are. This restores the individualistic beliefs and perspective you have of life by realizing that everyone is interconnected and dependent on one another. The competitive, selfish and narcissistic ways will begin to fade because you now know that your actions affect your partner, family members, friends and colleagues.

DAILY GRATITUDE EXERCISE

Gratitude can only become a habit and part of your personality once you put in the work at least once every day. Here are a few options you may consider adding to your to-do list (Mayor Galindo, 2021):

- **Visualize three to five things you are grateful for**

Name three to five things you feel thankful for, visualize it and write it down. Do not rush to come up with things to mention, take at least 10 minutes of your time to focus on what you are thankful for. At the end of each week, go back to the page you wrote what you are thankful for and read it again. By doing this exercise every day, you automatically set the tone for a good day ahead.

- **Purchase a gratitude journal**

Gratitude journals are often used as part of self-therapy. When you write what you feel thankful for, you are using many regions of the brain. You are thinking about past memories, emotions come into play and happy thoughts are associated with it. It is believed that once you can see the positive in a negative situation, you are able to show resilience, forgiveness and detachment. Also, on days when you feel under the weather, going back to read what you wrote in the journal will uplift you.

- **Express gratitude toward a different person every week**

Assign yourself the task to thank someone in your life every week. Thank your mother for her endless love, your partner for cooking dinner, a colleague for their help and so forth. This allows you to redirect the focus that is always on yourself to others. By expressing how grateful you are to someone different each week will teach you different ways of showing gratitude. Each person differs and your relationship with each one differs as well therefore your approach to expressing gratitude will also be different. You may try verbally thanking someone, writing a letter, or buying a gift to show gratitude.

- **Recognize the efforts of others**

Try to focus your attention on how others are lighting up your life. Whenever you recognize someone is being kind toward you, thank them. Acknowledge how they are trying to make you smile or to support you in your time of need.

- **Meditate**

You are aware of how meditation works as you learned about it in chapter two. However, in this chapter meditating slightly differs as the purpose for it changes. Here you will use the time during meditation to reflect on the things you are grateful for and imagine specific memories that you are thankful you got to experience.

Whichever technique you use, here are a few tips to help you make the most of practicing gratitude:

- Ask your friends or family to engage in a gratitude exercise with you. For example, before having dinner each one is required to name three things they are grateful for.

- As a narcissist, it will be easy to forget to practice gratitude. Set a reminder on your phone, paste a gratitude sticker on your desk at work or the fridge at home or tell someone about wanting to make gratitude a habit and ask them to check up everyday if you engaged in a gratitude exercise.

- Once you have completed a gratitude practice such as writing in your journal and thanking someone in person, do not just jump to your next task. Try to ponder on the moment for about 15 seconds.

- When writing in a gratitude journal (or just on a piece of paper what you are grateful for), avoid writing "I am grateful for my partner"; instead, write, "I appreciate and feel thankful that my partner gives me back rubs whenever I get home at night." Try to be more specific when naming what you are grateful for.

Saying thank you at first might be hard, as you have a justified reason in mind there is no need to thank another person for their efforts. Below you will find five steps on how to thank someone authentically instead of just saying "thank you" without truly meaning it.

How to Authentically Say Thank You

Step one: Search for a reason why you want to thank someone.

Step two: Try to align your way of saying thank you with social rules.

Step three: Add a personal touch when saying thank you.

Step four: State why you are thankful and why it's important to you.

Step five: Be honest and sincere when thanking someone.

Switch From Apologizing to Expressing Gratitude

Can you remember when you last apologized to someone and truly meant it? You may say sorry in times when you realize your partner is on the verge of leaving. However, you are only apologizing so that you do not lose the person and there is no sincerity behind your "I'm sorry, my love!" In other situations, you may be wrong and someone would point it out, but you will blame it on them for making you behave in a certain way or making a mistake. Learn to make amends in an authentic manner. Chances are if you have narcissistic personality disorder you have hurt people in a cruel way. Jamgochian (n.d.) claims that when we switch from apologizing to expressing gratitude, we increase warmth and positive feelings, allowing us to connect deeper to the person on the receiving end. In this way, your partner or the person confronting you will feel that you care and show a willingness to want to correct the situation. Moreover, this is how you maintain relationships and solve problems without hurting someone and ending an argument with feelings of distress or causing damage to the relationship. Take the word "but" out of your vocabulary and stop defending yourself all the time.

Here is how to sincerely apologize to someone:

1. Before approaching the person, accept that you were wrong and remind yourself that it is okay to be wrong. Try not to let your inflated self-esteem, pride and egocentric ways get in the way. Remember you want to heal and mend broken relationships in your life. Make a mental note that this is not about you but about the other person who you have hurt with your actions and

when you try to apologize you are attempting to correct the situation.

2. Make the reason for apologizing clear. When you approach the person, start off by stating the main reason why you are speaking to them and what the conversation will entail. You need to know if the person is in the right mind space to deal with whatever you want to apologize for. Sometimes the other person does not have the emotional capacity to deal with the hurt all over again and you need to be okay with that. Just try again on a different occasion.

3. Admit to the person that you were wrong. If you see that it is okay to continue the conversation, start off by admitting that your behavior or actions were wrong and unacceptable. Let the person know that you are taking responsibility for your wrongs and that you are able to be accountable.

4. Recognize how the person at the receiving end might be feeling. Place yourself in their shoes and imagine how what you have done has hurt them. Let them know that you are aware of how your actions have led them to feel sad, hurt or angry. tap into your empathic side and understand where they are coming from instead of shifting the blame on them or being insensitive by brushing it off like you didn't hurt their feelings. Where your normal reaction would have been "I didn't hurt you, you are doing this to yourself," you

will respond with "I understand why you feel this way."

5. Sincerely apologize to the person. Keep your verbal apology simple and do not add any "but"s to your sentence.

6. Ask the person at the receiving end to forgive you. Ask them if there is anything you can do to rectify the situation and let them know that your relationship with them is important. Lastly, do not force them to forgive you by getting angry when they give you the cold shoulder.

IMPROVING PERSONALITY

Practicing gratitude will not only benefit and make the other person feel good, it also provides you with happiness as you appreciate having someone in your life that shows you kindness and love without having to ask for it or someone with malicious intentions. Let's have a look at five ways gratitude will benefit your narcissistic personality:

- Gratitude improves your mental health. According to Fulton (2020), a study done in 2020 proved that the practice of gratitude eases symptoms of anxiety and depression while another study done in 2013 claims that it also improves your mood. Anxiety and depression are sometimes comorbid with narcissistic personalities due to people not living up to their expectations, insecurities, and the lonely feeling as a result of pushing people away with your narcissism. A happier mood and positive internal environment makes room for healing to take place, a willingness to want to improve yourself and you will be a better person in relationships.

- Gratitude adds a positive element to all your relationships. By practicing gratitude, it means you are showing interest in another person which allows for your partner to feel satisfied and increases the overall vibe within the romantic relationship. Expressing gratitude toward others shows that you can reciprocate their energy and recognize when they are being kind. For this reason, more people will start to like you and improve the quality of your relationships. A direct consequence of healthy relationships leads to a bigger support group that you can rely on.

- Gratitude teaches you to be empathic and to be less aggressive. Individuals who practice gratitude are prosocial and follow social rules. When others seem to trigger the urge to become aggressive, you will remain level-headed. For example, when you receive negative feedback from someone at work or from your significant other, you will be empathic toward them instead of catering to your bruised ego. You will understand why they are saying what they said without feeling offended by it. You will not be phased by criticism because your ability to be grateful will find the positive out of the feedback you got. Instead of feeling like "They are hurting my feelings" by the feedback they provided, your mindset will shift to "What lessons can I take from the feedback to improve myself?"

- Gratitude will help you to have a realistic and optimal level of self-esteem. Gratitude is known to increase self-esteem but for a narcissist, it will help you realize that you are a normal individual, like everyone else meaning it will bring your level of self-esteem to an optimal level. Gratitude reduces your narcissistic tendency of making social comparisons and helps you to treat people as equally. This will help you to be less envious of others and to be happy for others' achievements as well as mingle with groups that differ from you.

- Gratitude improves your ability to handle difficult mental strains and traumas. Cultivating a thankful attitude toward others and life in general, increases mental strength. Your mental strength will build your resilience toward mental strains and stressful events as well as help you overcome traumas. Gratitude will help you find the silver lining and the lessons from traumas you have endured. In addition, pain from parental neglect, constant criticism and traumas from childhood can be decreased. This will help to let go of insecurities, the need for external validation, entitlement and being envious.

4

FOCUSING OUTWARDS

By now you are aware of most of your narcissistic traits and behaviors that are toxic and causing your relationships to sink. You are in the process of learning how to rewire your brain and how you respond to the world. The previous chapter encouraged you to be grateful instead of believing that everything you have is because of you and your efforts. It helped you acknowledge that all humans are interconnected and interdependent; thus without each other, nobody can move forward or be successful. In this chapter, you are motivated to focus on your external world and not to be fixated on yourself and your inner world. You tend to make every situation about yourself and refuse to give credit to your external sources. Life is not just about you; there are millions of other people to share earth with. Ralph Waldo Emerson states that "The purpose of life is not to be happy. It is to be useful, to be honorable, to be compassionate, to have it make some difference that you have lived and lived well" (Excellence Reporter, 2019). With that being said, being happy and boosting your ego is not top priority in life. Exploiting and manipulating people to get what you want is not having a positive impact on the world. However, you should be able to extend a helpful hand to others without expecting anything in return, help make the world a better place and radiate positive energy. The difference you want to make is not negative, but positive, right? Therefore you need to get out of your head, and focus your attention on the people and things around you.

Being self-absorbed and thinking you are not dependent on the people around you puts pressure on the self and leads to worsening your personality disorder. This chapter will teach you how to be less self-absorbed and how to be compassionate instead of boastful. Being egotistical will be a downfall and a negative trait that will push others away and result in poor relationships. The efforts you want from others should be reciprocated. What you wish to receive from the world should also be given from you to the world. You will also learn to shift your focus on the meaning and purpose of your life and lastly, find new ways to respond. Oftentimes, you respond with malicious intent, schemes and using manipulative tactics to get through life and to benefit from as well as ignore the needs of others in the process. However, learning a new way to respond helps you to cultivate healthier and higher quality relationships which also add to your journey of rewiring the brain to improve your personality.

LETTING GO OF SEEKING APPROVAL

Someone who is self-absorbed is hyper focused on themselves, and shows little to no interest in others. They come across as selfish because they only care about getting what they want and disregard the feelings of others. They do not care whether it hurts or inconveniences others, as long as they get what they want. Being self-absorbed, egotistical, boastful and attention-seeking are one of the most prominent elements of being a narcissist. You always need to get validated and seek approval from others. When you buy a new car, it gets posted online so that people can comment and like your post. You might go as far to visit friends and family you never visit just to show them the car, fishing for compliments. While this is how most people operate in the modern world by being flashy and posting about your life, you take it to the extreme and depend on others' comments to feed your ego and make you feel good about yourself. What if I told you there is a way to validate yourself and make yourself feel good without the approval of others? Would you be willing to try it? Would you be able to give up both negative and positive approval?

When you let go of seeking attention and approval from others, the anxiety and fear of not getting approval will no longer be an issue to you. Once you get it right, heal from past trauma and pain, and successfully reprogram your brain, you will realize that seeking validation from others is not as important as you currently make it out to be. From a young age, you have learned through social conditioning that elevating yourself, being successful and impressing others will be a technique to gain approval and validation. This is not healthy to our internal environment as it causes distress when we don't get the validation and approval that we expect. Also, you will start to abandon yourself to please others. Edberg (2021) claims that when you shift the spotlight and care less about what others say by coming across as less self-absorbed, you will gain freedom inside your mind to actually take the focus off yourself and develop a genuine interest for what the other person is saying.

An essential part of improving your personality entails working on the traits that causes you to fall at the higher end of the narcissistic spectrum. The trait you will be working on is becoming less self-absorbed. Below is some tips to help you decrease your level of being self-absorbed and develop an interest in the lives of others:

- Treat others with the same love and respect you expect from them. Think about how you would feel if someone treated you in a self-absorbed way and not caring about your feelings. If their behavior riled you up, then it shows that your behavior is problematic and should be changed.

- Try to comprehend the perspective of another person. You are so caught up in how you feel that you fail to acknowledge or want to understand the view of another individual. Remember, everyone's perspective is influenced by their past experiences and so is yours.

This means not everyone's opinion will match yours and you must be okay with someone disagreeing with you.

- Be generous and offer help even if it does not benefit you in any way. For example, if you are about to make yourself a cup of coffee, offer to make some for the rest of your family or your partner as well. Do not get up, boil some water and come back with a cup of coffee. Even if they decline your offer, at least you have made the effort to perform a kind gesture.

- Take timing into consideration. Do not feel discouraged or angry when someone rejects your offer to help or does not seem grateful for your kind gesture. Consider the feelings and mental state of the person. Before making assumptions, try to understand what the other person is experiencing at that moment. Therefore, you should make the effort to stay up to date with what's happening in the lives of your loved ones.

- Start by making small changes in your relationships with others. Making big changes at the start of your journey to improving your personality may feel too hard and your efforts may backfire. You should be mindful of how you will come across to others when you are on your healing journey as they might perceive you as mistrustful especially because you have hurt them in the past. Also, make sure that you are consistent with whatever change you are about to make within the relationship. An example of a small change may refer to letting your partner choose where to go on your next date night as you are always the one to pick the place. You will start being less controlling and allow your partner to make decisions as well.

- Work on your listening skills. If you are self-absorbed, chances are that you have difficulty seeing beyond your own view. Improving how you communicate with your loved ones can be a stepping stone for great relationships to evolve. Communication in a relationship is a two-way street. Both parties should be active participants, willing to hear each other out with empathy and compassion. No relationship should be one-sided when it comes to communication. However, by now you must have realized all the relationships you find yourself in become one sided because you want to take up all the space in the relationship. Ziogas (2021) states that active listening is a transformative skill and it doesn't just negate your need to speak, it also removes your strict hold of the world revolving around you. Listen attentively, make them feel seen and heard. Do not respond because you are obligated to, respond with love and kindness. Also, avoid sharing personal stories or advice when someone is venting to you.

- Take a walk in someone else's shoes. When you deal with your own issues, you tend to project how you feel onto others as well as expect others to sympathize with you. If you experience a problem, you feel other people's problems are not bigger or more painful than yours. This is why you need to force yourself into taking a walk in someone else's shoes in order to understand what they are experiencing. Remind yourself that other people all have traumas and pain they are processing.

- Not every comment toward you needs a reaction. You have such a fragile ego that it can bruise easily therefore you lash out in the event that someone makes a snide comment about you. Try not to take everything personal and learn to let it go. What people see is a projection of who they are and does not necessarily accurately reflect you. It is most likely that you will react impulsively and say things that could have been avoided.

- Being selfish and self-absorbed becomes a habit that every time you engage it you are feeding a perpetual cycle. This makes it harder to break. The only way to break the habit of being selfish and self-absorbed is to learn new and healthier habits that will replace the old and unwanted ones.

- To focus outwards and develop an interest in others, it is suggested that you find ways to make life easier for the ones around you. For example, volunteering at a community center or spending a day at a children's home. The more generous acts you do for others out of love, the more the focus will turn toward a collectivistic perspective instead of focusing on yourself.

- Lastly, keep track of your progress. Write down when you are practicing being less self-absorbed and selfish. In this way you will be able to see which new habits, beliefs and attitudes you have adopted. In addition, you will be able to see which behaviors still need improvement.

To rewire your brain to respond differently to triggering feelings, you need to learn new responses such as counting to 10, doing a body scan, grounding yourself and breathing techniques. Here is a simple grounding technique to practice: name five things you can see, four things you can feel, three things you can hear, two things you can smell and one thing you can taste. You may use this technique when you feel triggered, so that you distract the mind from automatically responding in narcissistic ways.

SELF-COMPASSION OVER SELF-PROMOTION

It is common for a narcissist to brag and promote their achievements, material possession or flaunt their looks. In the modern world, self-promotion is on the rise with all the social media platforms who provide people with the opportunity to do so. Narcissistic behavior is so easy to engage in lately as the world revolves around Instagram, WhatsApp, Snapchat, Facebook, TikTok, YouTube, etc. Whenever someone gets a new pair of shoes, they post a photo in it and create clothing hauls for TikTok and YouTube. Grandiose narcissists tend to expose their lifestyle all over social media such as post the parties they attend, the food and wine they indulge in, pictures of cars they drive and so forth. The amount of likes and followers a narcissist has may contribute to their inflated self-esteem and irrational sense of self-importance. However, vulnerable narcissists are introverted and are not the type to frequently post online. Promoting yourself is not negative but it becomes unhealthy when you start exaggerating the truth and putting others down to boost your ego.

To positively affirm the self, it suggested that you engage in self-compassion instead of self-promotion. Self-compassion comes from kindness while self-promotion comes from the ego. Self-compassion is defined as treating yourself with warmth and empathy when you feel inadequate, inferior, or like a failure. Self-compassion helps you to avoid beating yourself up, engaging in unhealthy coping mechanisms, repressing the pain to minimize feeling inadequate, inferior or like a failure. When you experience a setback, you often become defensive, try to put the blame on others or belittle yourself in which none of these methods are healthy ways of dealing with the situation. It might alleviate the feeling that comes with the experience of the setback, but it does not teach you anything. Research suggests that in such situations one should resort to self-compassion (Chen, 2018). By using self-compassion, it means you are demonstrating the following behaviors:

- When you slip up or fail at something, you are not judgmental toward yourself. You are able to be kind to yourself by reframing your thoughts.

- You believe failing is part of life and it is inevitable that you will make mistakes because it is how you learn and grow as an individual.

- You allow yourself to feel bad about making a mistake, but you do not dwell on it for too long to the extent that it starts controlling your mood and behavior.

By being self-absorbed, you tend to compare yourself with others that you encounter which makes room for jealousy and envy to wash over you. Self-compassion cultivates a growth mindset—a mindset that will allow you to vibrate higher and to get closer to your ideal self. When you are self-compassionate, you choose not to avoid judging yourself and others, especially on days when you are feeling under the weather due to something hurtful you said, or an error you made at work. However, self-compassion helps you improve your sense of self-worth.

Moreover, having a high self-esteem and categorizing yourself as above others causes you to become complacent while believing you are the black swan and below everyone causes you to become pessimistic and insecure. You need to find the right balance by accepting your authentic self without exaggerating by becoming self-compassionate. When you practice self-compassion, you will be able to work on your weaknesses and provide realistic self-appraisals. Also, self-compassion leaves room for evolving your being. Some narcissists may have a fixed mindset while others don't. For example, they might believe that their traits are fixed and who they are now is who they will be forever. But there is also the type of narcissist who wants to improve (like you). However, it is highly unlikely that a narcissist wants to change.

As for the narcissist who wants to improve and enhance their personality, fostering self-compassion will not be easy but it will be a worthwhile task. Chen (2018) suggests using a three-point checklist by asking yourself the following questions:

- Am I being kind and understanding to myself?

- Do I acknowledge shortcomings and failure as experiences shared by everyone?

- Am I keeping my negative feelings in perspective?

If the three-point checklist didn't do the trick, try to write a short letter addressed to yourself. For this task, you need to pretend to be a caring, loving and warm person toward someone who is going through a hard time. What will you say to make them feel better? What would you want someone to tell you when you need a little support? In the letter you need to show yourself unconditional love and positive regard. By doing this, you will avoid flagellation.

COMPASSION AS A HABIT

In this section, we have created an easy practice for you to make compassion a habit. This habit will replace your need for self-promoting in which compassion will be the tool that soothes your insecurity and fragile ego as well as treat others in a kinder manner. Instead of focusing on thoughts that creates a barrier between you and others, compassion will slowly break down this barrier and help you to focus your attention outwards by showing interest and love. Remember habits are formed over time and by being consistent. It is suggested that you practice compassion before you are about to interact with someone or before leaving your house for work.

Here are three easy steps to make compassion a habit:

1. Step one is to become aware of your thoughts and feelings.

Once you come in contact with people, for example at the train station, grocery store, at work, or a social event you must notice what your thoughts are telling you and what your internal environment feels like. You may start to observe people and already decide not to socialize with them because you believe you are better than them. Use your innate response as a cue to know you should be compassionate.

2. When you feel the lack of compassion in you, consciously shift.

Your normal response would be to leave the event if it is not up to your standard. For instance, you leave the meeting at work, you hang up the phone or leave your sister's birthday party because you are not the most dominant and not treated as important. However, step two encourages you to make the shift by simply sending the ones you are about to meet up with a kind message. You could say a phrase like "hope you are doing well" either in your mind or out loud. Saying in your mind and genuinely meaning it will cause you to feel blissful and warm on the inside. To enhance the feeling you should say it to the person you are meeting.

3. Let the feeling marinade.

The last step wants you to think about how you handled the situation with compassion and to savor the moment for about 30 seconds. Let the feeling sink in and bathe yourself in the goodness of compassion. Allowing the feeling to sink, will cause the brain to learn a new way of responding to situations that you would innately use narcissistic tendencies. Then compare this feeling to the feeling you normally feel after you leave an event or hang up because things aren't going your way. Do you feel the difference? Which one makes your internal environment feel better?

MEANING AND PURPOSE

The meaning and purpose of life differs from person to person. Martinez & Alayan (2021) define meaning in life as a feeling that one's life is significant, purposeful, and coherent; in other words, having a direction that makes sense and has a feeling of worth. What you see as a meaningful life is closely connected to your personal values. These values are beliefs that you deem as important and drive your actions. Also, living a meaningful life has benefits that include a happier state of mind and high quality relationships. Purpose, on the other hand, is the goal we have set for ourselves to achieve that we will devote our whole life to. Our purpose is tied to a need to make a positive impact on the world. For instance, choosing a career that will benefit the mental health of others by becoming a therapist or a doctor to make sure people's physical health are on par. But note that your purpose can change as you grow and start developing new ways of seeing the world. When we live our purpose, it makes life meaningful.

A more general view of the meaning and purpose of life could be seen as pure love. Our soul purpose of life is to love and when we are able to give and receive love, life becomes meaningful. Love is known to heal all wounds and creates a safe space for you to be your best self. When our actions are all derived from love, our intentions toward others become pure and genuine. Once you focus on your purpose and allow it to bring meaning to your life, you will realize that there is no need for being manipulative, envious, self-absorbed, or controlling. Focus on meaning and purpose instead of focusing on status driven activities like social likes or the car you drive. This will improve relationships with others because you will be able to converse about topics that act in the best interest of everyone, not just your own. Discussing your passion and interests with others, without looking for a compliment or positive affirmations from them will change their perspective of you in a good way.

Your narcissistic personality may have shifted your focus from your true purpose in life. Try to remember why you are placed on this earth, how you can make the world a better place by being in it and which actions you should take to achieve it. Here are a few tips to keep you focused on your purpose:

1. Align your energy with your purpose as soon as you wake up.

Every morning you need to at least use 30 minutes of your time to shift your focus on your soul purpose. This will set the tone for the day and help you behave in alignment with your purpose.

2. Only do activities that are aligned with your purpose.

After step one, try your best to ensure that every move you make is driven by your purpose. Remember, your purpose refers to something that adds positivity and fruitfulness to the world. Meaning you will engage in less narcissistic behaviors and act in a way that benefits others and not yourself.

3. Take time during the day to check in and regain perspective.

Even though you have set the tone for the day to be aligned with your purpose, minor issues can throw you off and make you go back to engaging in narcissistic behaviors. When you feel yourself slipping into old habits, try to step back, breathe and refocus your mind on your purpose.

4. Make a habit out of asking yourself, *What do I want?*

Frequently ask yourself what you want in order to grow and develop in ways that aligns with your purpose. As a narcissist, you want to change your ways and rebuild/maintain relationships in your life, then your actions need to align with becoming a better version of yourself so that you are a healthier person in your personal relationships. If what you are doing is not working, ask yourself *What do I want?* and go after it.

5. Set goals to keep you motivated to live your purpose.

In order to constantly be aligned with your purpose and to ensure that you are living it, consistently set goals that resonate with it. If your purpose is to be a better person in your romantic relationship, your goal might be to work on being less self-absorbed and dominant.

6.   At the end of each day, journal about it.

To stay aligned with your purpose, reflect upon your day every night. In this way you determine if you have lived your purpose for the day, what you have experienced and what lessons you have learned. On some days, you may have worked less on pursuing your purpose, but that does not mean you should beat yourself up. It means the following day, you can make up for it.

5

COGNITIVE
BEHAVIORAL THERAPY

What is your go-to strategy when you are dealing with life? Do you engage in healthy coping mechanisms to self-regulate? Narcissists are known to indulge in unhealthy coping mechanisms such as drug and alcohol abuse to numb the sting of their problems. Besides these coping mechanisms being unhealthy, it does not address the main problem of your personality disorder. In this chapter, we make use of cognitive behavioral therapy techniques to tackle the root of your problems. People with personality disorders, particularly narcissistic personality disorder, experience distorted thoughts that negatively affect their behavior which invites problems into their relationships and personal life. Cognitive behavioral therapy is a recommended therapy for personality disorders as it can address a variety of complex problems ranging from maladaptive thoughts to unhealthy behaviors.

Narcissists do not always progress well during therapy because they become manipulative, difficult, and defensive which makes it hard to treat them. Some may want to be in control and steer the conversation instead of allowing the therapist to do their job. Here is a therapist describing their experience working with a narcissist, Richard (Behary, 2013):

He often shifted into self-aggrandizing monologues on his latest brilliant investment, his newly purchased, one-of-a-kind this or that, his powerful business connections, his to-die-for wine collection. Whenever I hazarded an insight into his childhood or suggested that he might be feeling scared, he tried to derail me by saying something like, "I took some psychology classes, too, you know, and I could have been a great therapist." When talking about his marital problems, he'd say, "My wife has PMS. That's the problem, not me. You have no idea what I have to put up with and all that I do to make her happy. But it's never good enough."

When our conversations ventured toward emotionally loaded material, he shifted into detached mode, denying that he had any feelings. When I tried to get him to see that this is a way of protecting himself from feeling difficult emotions, he demeaned me for my "hokey-pokey, touchy-feely therapy" that had "no relevance" to him. Rolling his eyes, he'd proclaim that he had a perfectly fine childhood and that the only reason for us to look at his past is to satisfy my need to justify myself as a therapist who's charging a hefty fee.

Cognitive behavioral therapy focuses on three aspects: thoughts, affect and behavior. By now you have raised your self-awareness and have insight into how your narcissistic personality developed without the help or guidance of a therapist. Accepting the reasons might be hard, but it is important to let go of denial if you want your healing journey to be successful. Moreover, chapter five will educate you on what cognitive behavioral therapy is, the steps you can expect to take, and how it improves your narcissistic tendencies. The second part of the chapter focuses on the various techniques that you can use to improve yourself while the last section discusses the benefits of the therapy.

What is Cognitive Behavioral Therapy?

Cognitive behavioral therapy is defined as a blend of cognitive and behavioral therapy. This therapy sheds light on how one's thoughts and beliefs become the motivation behind how one behaves and how they feel. According to *Treating Narcissistic Personality Disorder With CBT* (2015) cognitive behavioral therapy is practical and technique-based, with "homework" assignments that help patients immediately put to use the skills they have learned in therapy. By using cognitive behavioral therapy you will be focusing on current problems and solving them with meaningful strategies. Cognitive behavioral therapy will challenge core beliefs that are the cause of narcissistic behaviors while identifying automatic and maladaptive interpretations of your environment (*Cognitive-Behavioral Therapy for Personality Disorders (CBT)*, n.d.). When you correct those core beliefs, you develop new beliefs and new ways of interpreting your environment. You will be required to identify problems, recognize how your thoughts play a role in destructive behaviors and to change them by replacing distorted thoughts with rational and healthy thoughts.

Below we unpack the steps you can expect when using cognitive behavioral therapy techniques:

1. Step one requires you to recognize in which domains of your life you experience problems. There may be various problems that pop up but the main problem we are addressing is your need to control people, being abusive, and your troublesome relationships.

2. In step two you need to identify how you feel about the problem above as well as your thoughts and beliefs about it. You may create a document or write on a page. Make three columns in which you report your thoughts, feelings and beliefs about the problem. In this way, you are able to gain more insight on the problem.

3. Step three wants you to make use of the document or page created in step two to identify any negative or inaccurate thinking. This step might be difficult because it may be hard for you to see any faults. One

technique to use refers to pretending to be a friend of yourself, placing yourself outside of the problem and then interpreting the problem again. Another way to do this is, working with a trusted friend or family member to help you recognize unhealthy patterns of thinking and behavior.

4. In the last step, you will attempt to reframe the inaccurate thought patterns. Ask yourself, *Are my thoughts, beliefs, and feelings based on facts, or are they influenced by my narcissistic personality*? This is how you will challenge and change your thoughts which will automatically transform your behavior and mood.

IMPROVING NARCISSISTIC BEHAVIOR

In this section, we only discuss the cognitive behavioral therapy techniques that will decrease narcissism. All the techniques have a goal of transforming thoughts and emotions that hinder your mental state which urges you to engage in narcissistic tendencies as well as altering behaviors that negatively affect yourself and those around you. The techniques you will be introduced to below will improve your thought patterns, enhance your mood and increase effective behavior.

Cognitive Reframing

Cognitive reframing is also known as cognitive restructuring which can be defined as a technique one uses to identify unhealthy thought patterns and to modify them into accurate, realistic and grounded ones. This technique helps you to interpret situations for what it is, instead of what you want them to be. How we interpret situations largely depends on our backgrounds, life experience, personality and society to name a few factors. In your case, your brain is wired to interpret the world with a narcissistic mindset. However, we all make use of mental shortcuts to make sense of our worlds. It becomes unhealthy when the brain automatically uses a shortcut that does not apply to the situation at hand. This is when we start labeling the mental shortcut as a cognitive distortion in which our thoughts become distorted and unhealthy, and our interpretation of the world becomes skewed.

COGNITIVE DISTORTIONS

It is as the result of cognitive distortions that narcissists strongly believe what they feel and have the inability to see the reality of the situation. Cognitive distortions may be your way of making sense of a situation but keeps you stuck in negative situations or worsen the problem. People with narcissistic personality disorder commonly use the following cognitive distortions which explains why they are pessimistic, feel entitled and destroy others mentally (Shaw, 2019):

- All or nothing thinking

You think in black and white, leaving no space for gray areas to occur which means you expect everything to go one of two ways. You think of yourself as the most perfect being; anything that does not match your level of perfection is sent to the left. This explains why you only choose to associate with certain people, only go attend certain events, and leave as soon as something is not to your liking. Also, because you believe you are the most perfect and smartest person, you tend to place the blame on others or project your failures onto others.

- Jumping to conclusions

As a narcissist, you love to inaccurately read other people's minds. You might claim to be a great judge of character and believe the thoughts you have about someone which could be completely false and imprecise. What you think and how you feel are not always based on facts therefore you cannot jump to conclusions and act upon it. Due to the belief that you think you know how others operate makes you show a lack of interest in finding out the truth, so you go with the version of the story that your false mind created. This tells us why you gaslight and invalidate the feelings of others.

- Catastrophizing

This cognitive distortion describes your thought patterns and behavior in two ways. Firstly, you tend to minimize your actions when you hurt the feelings of another by telling them "You are too sensitive" and secondly, you magnify your good qualities to impress others. You may see the correlation between using catastrophizing and when you receive criticism as well. When being criticized you exaggerate the magnitude of the comment and allow it to trigger your aggressive side. Also, this explains why you minimize the efforts of others and tend to be unappreciative.

- Negative filtering

Negative filtering darkens your mind and blinds you to positivity in situations. When you have an argument with someone, you filter out all the positive things and only focus on the negative that were said. Furthermore, you take the negative and twist it to fit your narrative by using the negative information to shift the blame and proceed to gaslight. At the end you apologize by saying, "I'm sorry, but if you didn't do that, I wouldn't have reacted in that way."

- Always right

As a consequence of all or nothing thinking, lacking the ability to reflect and being self-absorbed, you believe you are always right. Once you have made up your mind about something, you stick to it. You will go to great lengths to show someone that you are in fact right by using manipulative tactics. In addition, to you being right is more important than the feelings of another person. Because you lack empathy, you will hurt them, emotionally damage them or pick a fight just to show that you are right. Someone may disagree with you and give you their interpretation of an event to show that your version of the event is inaccurate. This is when you choose to invalidate their perception and make them experience cognitive dissonance. You make them question themselves where you are at fault.

- Personalization

This type of cognitive distortion is the reason why you make everything about yourself and always want to be the main character. You start gaining a sense of entitlement as a result of this mindset. Your personality and mind becomes pessimistic as you start to treat others with this attitude in which you only care about getting your needs met even if it means you must be nasty to someone. For example, you are aware that someone is struggling financially but you still demand that they pay you for giving them a lift from work to the bus stop on a rainy day. Moreover, personalization makes you believe that every action of another person is directed at you. You will start to believe that someone else's success is because you helped them in the past or feel a comment made by a colleague walking past is aimed at you.

- Should

Be honest with yourself and ask, *Why do I want to change?* Shaw (2019) states that a narcissist might think that they should change, yet this only occurs in a moment when they are not getting something they want. Do you want to change because you are lonely or because you truly want to mend the relationships in your life? Oftentimes narcissists make empty promises as wanting to change is a temporary decision. Once you get what you want, you take your decision back and return to your old ways. After an argument with your partner you may think, *Maybe I should change to keep this relationship,* but after you love bombed your partner with gifts and are forgiven, you change the narrative by saying "You should change, then I won't behave in this way."

REFRAMING DYSFUNCTIONAL THOUGHT PATTERNS

A dark and pessimistic mindset that motivates your behavior to become harmful and cause damage to the lives of others can be reduced by restructuring those distorted and dysfunctional trains of thoughts. Use the following steps to reframe your thoughts:

1. Take a breather and bring yourself to a calm state of mind.

2. Write down the situation that causes the dysfunctional thinking to occur.

3. Try to identify the emotions that arise as a result of the situation.

4. Make a note of the automatic thoughts you experienced when you felt the emotion.

5. Identify the evidence that supports these thoughts.

6. Identify the evidence that contradicts the thoughts.

7. Compare the evidence that supports your thoughts with the ones that contradict it. This will help you to see whether your thoughts are accurate or false.

Behavioral Activation

Behavioral activation also known as activity scheduling is based on behavioral principles. Behaviorism is a theory that suggests our environment is a factor that drives our behavior as well as affects our mental health. Behavioral activation is a technique that motivates you to activate behaviors that will enhance your personality and mental health. Instead of behaving in ways that are seen as narcissistic, behavioral activation steers you in the direction of engaging behaviors that will enhance relationships.

Two reasons to make use of behavioral activation (Villines, 2021):

- Behavioral activation replaces narcissistic behaviors with healthier ones.
- Your modified behavior will lead to improved relationships.

PUTTING IT INTO ACTION

1. Identify how your actions influence your emotions. Step one usually wants you to compare behaviors that make you feel bad to the ones that make you feel good. However, in your case you are required to compare behaviors that are unhealthy to the ones that are healthy. This can be done by looking at the response of the person you want to mend a relationship with. If it hurts them, it is unhealthy and toxic behaviors which should be a signal that the behavior you presented should be modified. On the other hand, if the person reacts positively to certain behaviors, take it as a signal to increase those behaviors.

2. Once you figure out which behaviors to increase and which to modify, set a goal to work toward engaging more in these specific behaviors. Note that you should not bite off more than you can chew. Choose two behaviors and slowly practice it more often within the relationship. For example, before you would call your

partner "sensitive" during an argument for crying or want to control what they wear when you go on dates.

3. Replace the behaviors that need to be modified. Let's say you chose to change one of the two behaviors mentioned above, you would either start being a better listener or accept the clothes your partner chooses to wear. This might be difficult but remember the main goal is to increase behaviors that will have a positive impact on the relationship. Note that this should not be used as a manipulative tactic.

4. Record your progress and check if new behaviors are bringing positive change to your relationship as well as decrease your automatic response of engaging in narcissism.

Behavioral Experiments

Behavioral experiments is a cognitive behavioral therapy technique that allows you to test inaccurate and distorted thoughts or beliefs by conducting your own experiment. As a narcissist who struggles to see when you are wrong, jump to conclusions, and think in black and white, behavioral experiments can be a beneficial technique to help you see things from a realistic point of view. Holding onto outdated beliefs and inaccurate thoughts can lead to distress. For example, believing you are perfect and should always be perfect to impress others and for them to like you. People pleasing is unhealthy and will cause your mental health to decline as you tend to go to extreme lengths to please others even if it goes against your values. Eventually you start feeling disappointed in yourself when you fail to impress others. Here is a short example of a perfectionist who tried a behavioral experiment (Morin, 2020):

> A woman believes people will only like her if she is perfect. Her perfectionist tendencies create a lot of stress and anxiety. She agrees to conduct a behavioral experiment that involves making a few mistakes on purpose and then monitoring how people respond. She sends an email with a few typos and sends a birthday card with a grammatical error to see how people respond.

HOW TO DO A BEHAVIORAL EXPERIMENT

Here are seven steps to follow to successfully conduct a behavioral experiment:

Step 1: Identify which cognitive distorted or outdated belief you want to test.

Try to figure out which cognitive distortions or beliefs cause the most trouble in your life. Write the thought or belief down in one sentence. For example: "If I'm not the most dominant person in the relationship, I don't want the relationship."

Step 2: Rate how strongly you believe the thought or belief.

On a scale of 0 to 10, rate the strength of your thought or belief. 10 refers to strong while 0 refers to weak. You can also try to rate it with logic or with emotion. However, you as a narcissist are expected to rate what you believe and think as a 10 because you tend to view the thoughts that pop into your head as factual.

Step 3: Choose a method to do your behavioral experiment.

Brainstorm some ideas for how you will go about doing the experiment. Two methods that you can use to test your thought or belief refers to surveys and hypothesis-testing experiments. Method one requires you to ask others if they share the same thought or belief about a situation while method two asks you to guess the outcome of your experiment. Hypothesis-testing experiments will allow you to make a prediction about the experiment, for example: "If I do this, that will happen."

Step 4: Think about any challenges you might face during your experiment.

Ask yourself the following questions to gather information for step four:

- What are some obstacles that can arise in the process of conducting my experiment?

- If I choose to do surveys, who can I trust to be a participant?

- Is there any danger or possibility that I can worsen my narcissistic tendencies with this experiment? If so, what can I do to decrease the likelihood of it happening?

Step 5: Do your experiment.

Doing the experiment may sound easy but it will take much mental energy and push your limits or even trigger you. *How to use behavioural experiments to test what you believe* (n.d.) states that step five will require courage from your side. Sometimes during this step, you may get cold feet. You will start questioning the purpose of it as you believe you are always right so why does your thought or belief need to be tested? Well, this is the part where you need to remain focused on the main goal and getting closer to the finish line. You can ask someone to support and motivate you as well as remind you why you started the behavioral experiment in the first place.

Step 6: Write down the result of your experiment.

Recording the result of your experiment is essential to come to a conclusion. The result will be used to compare your thoughts or beliefs and to finally get an answer that will either prove you right or wrong.

Step 7: Use the results to form a conclusion.

Go back to step one and compare the outcome of the experiment with your initial thought or belief. Now repeat step two and rate how strongly you believe it. If you still strongly believe an inaccurate and distorted thought or belief, consider doing a follow-up experiment. However, if the experiment you conducted proves you wrong, it changes how you interpret the event and will decrease the belief that you are always right as you were provided with concrete evidence for example.

Journaling and Thought Records

As a narcissist, you find it difficult to do cognitive reflection and lack insight. One method to help you gain self-awareness and to recognize troubling behaviors and dysfunctional thoughts is to frequently write in a journal about your day or fill in thought records.

Skills Training

Most of the ways that you respond to situations are unhealthy because you do not have the skills or knowledge to know how to behave appropriately. Three areas that skills training focus on refers to developing your communication and social skills. One of the methods you can use for skills training is role play. However, you will need the help and guidance of someone you trust and are mentally stable because you need to model their behavior and be willing to take instructions from them. TheraNest Team (2020) claims role play helps clients to identify automatic thoughts, create new responses and practice them, and modify core beliefs as well as help to build problem-solving skills, improve communication skills, and boost social skills.

BENEFITS OF CBT FOR NARCISSISM

Cognitive behavioral therapy has many benefits as this kind of therapy is used widely by many therapists for many different conditions such as depression, anxiety, post traumatic stress disorder, and obsessive-compulsive disorder to name a few. There are many benefits to discuss when it comes to cognitive behavioral therapy but for the sake of this book, we will only look at four benefits as to how it improves your narcissism. Below we will unpack the four benefits (*What Are The Benefits Of Cognitive Behaviour Therapy (CBT)?*, 2019):

- Cognitive behavioral therapy provides you with a sense of hope that there is hope for you to improve your narcissistic behaviors. Before coming across this chapter, you might have been in a negative space mentally about the condition that your personal relationships are in and thought there is no way that you can change your ways in order to create healthy and long lasting connections with others. You have been with this personality for so long that you thought these traits that are holding you back have become fixed. Cognitive behavioral therapy allows you to see the silver lining and gives you hope that healthy relationships will be part of your future.

- Cognitive behavioral therapy helps grandiose and vulnerable narcissists to develop a healthy level of self-esteem. Both types of narcissists have difficulty when it comes to self-esteem thus why cognitive behavioral therapy will benefit them. It will disrupt inaccurate and irrational thoughts. For example, you are hypersensitive to criticism. The thoughts that arise when you are being criticized may be harmful and inaccurate in which cognitive behavioral therapy assists in changing your perception and thought patterns toward criticism. As a result, you will be able to deal with criticism in a healthy manner that will not negatively impact your self-esteem. By doing this, you are changing outdated beliefs that were printed in the head. In addition, you will develop a sense of self-confidence and perception of yourself that you did not have before—an accurate and rational view of yourself.

- Cognitive behavioral therapy calms your internal environment. The behavioral techniques of cognitive behavioral therapy teaches you to respond in a healthier manner to your triggers by self-regulating. In most cases, it involves using relaxation techniques such as mindfulness meditation, breathing, yoga, etc., to calm yourself. These relaxation techniques soothe your internal environment in order to avoid engaging in impulsive and narcissistic behaviors.
- Cognitive behavioral therapy wires your brain to operate with accurate and rational thought processes. You will be able to take control of your thoughts and will less likely engage in automatic responses which causes relationships problems. As a narcissist, your automatic response may be to rudely interrupt your partner while they speak as a way to assert dominance. When you start making a habit of cognitive restructuring, your automatic responses will fade in which your thoughts will naturally become more rational.

6

REPARENTING THE INNER CHILD

Take a few seconds and reflect on your childhood by asking yourself, *What was my experience like as a child*? You may remember your childhood as happy and as if nothing traumatic happened. But, sometimes it is not just about the things that happened but what did not happen that could also cause trauma. Most of us picture a happy childhood because we think of our families as perfect because our parents always tried to make us happy and have our needs met. One theory is that our parents may have wounds and unknowingly passed it onto us who grew up with trauma woven into our personalities.

In the previous chapter, we focused on cognitive behavioral therapy that used behaviorism and cognitive theories while the concept of parenting your inner child is derived from Jungian theory. Carl Jung proposed the idea that your inner child has contributed to the development of the self. However, in the modern world, reparenting the inner child is part of many schools of therapy such as Gestalt and transactional analysis. We were all children once upon a time, the child in us never disappears—we carry it with us through all our developmental stages. We are never only an adult, because a part of us will always be a child. The adult and child version of yourself coexists in which one of two are more dominant than the other in certain situations. Depending on the situation, the inner child will have something to say or alert you. But, are you listening to the voice or alarm going off, are you ignoring it or totally oblivious to it?

Noticing the inner child is difficult because it is part of our subconscious. Your inner child is awakened when you are triggered by a situation that reminds you of trauma experienced during childhood. So until you heal your inner child, it will be controlling your behavior and thoughts. Sometimes we act in ways that are uncalled for, only to feel puzzled about our behavior later. As an adult, you may still throw a tantrum when you do not get what you want. However, as a narcissist you have learned that throwing tantrums gets you what you want and therefore you continue doing it within various situations for example, at work and in your relationships. Our inner child is still a part of us, begs to be seen and heard through our unconscious behaviors. Note that the inner child shouldn't always be associated with the bad side of your personality because when our inner child is happy and healthy, we become the most inspiring, creative and blissful beings. When the inner child is broken and wounded, it separates from all its good qualities and starts feeling distressed.

According to Jacobson (2017), working with your inner child refers to a process of self-discovery that helps you access the child you once were, along with the experiences and emotions that we as children were taught to repress. Chapter six will help you nurture and heal your inner child so that there is no need to protect yourself by being narcissistic. Reparenting yourself means relearning new ways of loving yourself, getting your own needs met and developing a healthier version of the self. In this chapter, we cover the following topics:

- How childhood wounds occur
- Steps to heal the inner child
- Extra tips to nurture and heal your inner child

ORIGINS OF CHILDHOOD WOUNDS

Thinking of trauma may never be associated with your childhood because you believe you were an innocent child and nothing bad happened to you. You remember a happier and less stressed or anxious version of yourself who maybe had many friends and play dates. Truth is, you do not need to endure extreme abuse to become traumatized. As children, we were fragile and sensitive because we are still developing a self, meaning whether you experienced minor or major trauma, it had an influence on the formation of the personality you now have as an adult. In a child's life, parents are the one who they depend on to have their needs met. Our parents were the people who helped us regulate our emotions. Do you remember getting hurt, crying or being sad and our parents started flooding us with love and care to ensure that we are okay. They would ask "Must I kiss it better?" when you fell, or totally distract you from a situation that made you sad by bribing you with treats. However, from a child's point of view, a parent wanting to help might be interpreted in a negative way. For example, a parent reaching out to regulate their emotions but not doing it properly because the parents may be very young and the child may see their way of attempting to help them as negligence. In addition, whatever a child believes about a situation becomes facts to them as they have a limited perspective.

Let's look at an example of someone who tries to make sense of her abandonment issues in relationships as an adult (*Inner Child Work: How to Heal By Reparenting Yourself*, n.d.):

Recently, I spoke to my Mom about our family relations. We talked about childhood trauma and inner child work, too. As she shared her childhood memories, she asked me if I wanted to know something about my early years. I asked about a possibly traumatic event that I'm unlikely to remember. Without hesitation, she said there was something that stuck with her until today. When I was around 10 months old, my dad drove my mom and me to grandma for a couple of weeks. Then, he went back to work. This was the first time in my life I haven't seen him for so long. When he finally came back, I was lying on the bed as my mom was dressing me. In that moment, I turned my head to look at him. My mom swears I recognized him — and became upset that he left us for so long. I started crying. I cried and cried, and then cried some more. I didn't want him to hold me for hours. I don't know if that particular event traumatized me. What I do know is that, as an adult, I struggle with abandonment issues. Particularly when I enter a romantic relationship, I immediately fear that I'll be rejected.

Now you may wonder, *Why would my own mind and body play me like this?* All aspects of our being are integrated where it all influences each other, working as a team. A child's psyche is fragile so when something small hurts their feelings, parents often want to stop the child from physically expressing their feelings of anger or sadness. When a child is angry or sad they are told, "Stop crying, you are not a baby anymore!" Crying is associated with bad behavior and shame while laughing and smiling is associated with good behavior in which the child eventually learns to hide their pain. This leaves the child feeling shameful in which they repress their feelings because they are scared of being scolded for their way of expressing themselves. The same rules are then applied to when a child experiences trauma. The child represses the memory of the trauma, pushes it far back into the unconscious and starts hiding this trauma from themselves as well. This is a method that tricks you into believing that you have overcome the pain, but that same trauma is what rules your world. The trauma that is never processed and the pain you feel are stuck in your body in which it manifests in your adult life through relationships and sabotaging behaviors that jeopardizes your happiness without your awareness. This is caused by an adult wrapped in childhood trauma. Deep down, the younger version of yourself is angry, hurt and disappointed.

The following is a list of signs that you may have a wounded inner child (Davis, 2020):

- You suspect that there is something wrong with you but cannot find the root cause.

- You always want to please others.

- You thrive and feel happy when you argue with someone or do rebel-like activities.

- You tend to hoard stuff and find it hard to let go of items and people.

- You become anxious when introduced to something unfamiliar.

- When it is time to set boundaries within relationships, you feel guilty.

- You are motivated to be a top achiever in everything you do as well as a perfectionist.

- You are a procrastinator who finds it difficult to start or finish a task.

- You constantly criticize yourself.

- It is hard for you to express how you feel.

- You are hyper conscious of your appearance.

- You have a lack of trust in others.

- You do your best to avoid being involved in drama.
- You have a deep rooted fear of being abandoned.

Life skills you were supposed to learn from your parents during childhood (Davis, 2020):

- **Love and respect**

Your parents should teach you how to be kind and compassionate toward yourself as well as to respect your values and beliefs. They should also teach you that it is okay to be wrong and correct your beliefs when they are skewed. If they do not, your behavior may become arrogant. In addition, you had to be taught to set boundaries and to know how to protect your peace by letting go of people instead of clinging to wrong relationships.

When it comes to socializing with others, parents should have taught you to love and respect your friends and strangers by being non-judgmental. Parents should teach and model behavior that reflects respect and acceptance for people who differ from you. In this way, as an adult you will not have a mindset that separates you from people who are not on your level. If parents failed to teach you love and respect, you grow up to disrespect others and force your beliefs upon them.

- **Self-belief and self-confidence**

Parents should teach children to believe in themselves in order to be able to stay motivated even when they have failed at getting something right. This will allow the child to become confident with their being and not to seek external validation to feel happy about themselves. If your parents did not teach you self-belief and self-confidence, you end up being an adult who makes mistakes and starts beating yourself up for it then going to others and expecting them to make you feel confident about yourself.

- **Emotional management**

If you can remember, parents never literally tell us how to regulate emotions. We usually learn how to manage emotions through social conditioning and modeling therefore, if parents never knew how to appropriately regulate their emotions, their children will not either. This leads to an adult who becomes controlled by their emotions for example, when you are angry you will not react logically but in a way that worsen the situation.

- **Good communication skills**

Communication skills are one of the most important skills a parent or caregiver can teach you. You were supposed to be taught how to listen and respond effectively during conversations as well as how to read body language. Davis (2020) claims that forming deep and lasting relationships becomes extremely difficult when communication skills are compromised by a lack of parenting. If you weren't taught how to effectively communicate with others, you develop into an adult who lacks the ability to respect the opinion of another and to know the basics of treating another person in social interactions.

Please note that as this chapter might refresh your memory on traumatic events, do not blame your parents or caregivers for the person you have developed into as an adult. As a default way of dealing with life, you may run to play the blame game. Do not use this card to justify your behavior in relationships and hurting others, for example, saying "I am like this because my parents didn't love me; take me as I am." Healing and nurturing the inner child does not require you to hyper focus on uncovering what your parents did wrong and being angry at them—do not stay away from the main goal. You are allowed to feel angry but process these feelings without involving your parents. Your parents or caregivers tried their best to give you the life they could afford to give you with what they knew at the time. If you have trauma as a result of their behavior, it was not done deliberately but also a consequence of their unconscious traumas. We learn from *Inner Child Work: How to Heal By Reparenting Yourself* (n.d.) that it is in the nature of human experience to suffer. Many people seek the parenting they did not receive from parents in other places and from other people yet always being left disappointed by sources they seek parenting from. Jacobson (2017) states that if you were taught to repress pain, you might run from good relationships rather than allow yourself to be hurt. However, you always end up feeling alone even when in relationships and surrounded by others because you feel your needs are not being met. The end result is always feeling lonely. This could be another reason why you become codependent in relationships. Make it your responsibility to evolve and rise above the suffering by reparenting your inner child. Only by then will you be an adult who honors your needs and cultivates healthy relationships.

HEALING THE INNER CHILD

In the 1970s, Dr. Lucia Capacchione introduced the concept of reparenting through her art therapy which focused on work that ensured that the inner child feels valued, loved and safe. Before getting to the main steps of healing and nurturing the inner child, we will look at various forms of reparenting. The following forms are usually used in psychotherapy (Davis, 2020):

- **Total Regression:** Total regression refers to a type of parenting that is seldomly used and originates from the transactional analysis theory. This theory analyzes how you socially interact with others to determine your communication style: for example, whether it is child-like, parent-like, or adult-like. In the process of total regression, the patient receives in-patient therapy in which the therapist lives with them for years in an institution. During this time, the therapist has a main goal of transforming the parent ego state of the patient.

- **Time-Limited Regression:** Time-limited regression is mostly used in cases of patients with schizophrenia and post traumatic stress disorder. Instead of living with the therapist, the client has to attend five 2-hour therapy sessions. In those sessions, the patient's inner child is nurtured in a structured manner.

- **Spot Reparenting:** Spot reparenting is a less intense form of therapy than the two previous types of reparenting we discussed. By using spot reparenting you focus on specific events that caused trauma.
- **Self-Reparenting:** Self-reparenting is the most popular and used method amongst the four forms of reparenting. This form of reparenting focuses on acknowledging and strengthening the positive aspects that you already possess. Also, with self-reparenting you are in full control, and it depends on you to reparent yourself in comparison to having a therapist as guide or "parent."

By deciding to heal the inner child, it means you are making the conscious decision to give yourself everything you emotionally need. The adult version of you befriends the inner child in a way that a parent and child would. Who other than yourself, will ever love and care for you more than yourself? You are the best person to reparent yourself instead of looking for the things you lack in romantic relationships, friendships, or in spiritual communities in which we believe it will save us. However, this only brings temporary relief because others can only nurse the inner child if they meet your expectations. In the instance where these people you have been depending on do not meet your expectations, wounds are scratched open and you start to bleed again. Thus, why you can rely on reparenting yourself to heal insecurities and having a need to protect your being against everyone.

The main goal of working with your inner child is putting in the effort to connect, listen and nurture it in order to heal deep rooted traumas that sabotage your relationships during adulthood. While there are many ways you can go about healing your inner child, the following three steps are mandatory in the process:

Step one: Acknowledge and connect with the inner child

Before you can work with the inner child, you need to recognize its existence that is integrated with the adult self. This step is often quite challenging as it is similar to doing shadow work. You need to shed light on parts of the self that have been hidden, repressed and kept in the dark—might even be forgotten in the dark. Also, dealing with the discovery of old and painful memories will be hard and overwhelming so you need to mentally prepare for unwanted memories that will surface. Moreover, Richard Barrett's theory of psychological development states that as humans we need physical safety and a sense of acceptance and belonging to survive (*Inner Child Work: How to Heal By Reparenting Yourself*, n.d.). When parents fail to meet those needs during childhood, you spend your life as an adult wanting to satisfy and comfort those needs.

Okay, let's get practical. For step one you are required to get to know the younger version of yourself. Try to remember every detail of your childhood by asking yourself the following few questions:

- Did I stay in one location or move a lot?

- Did I have a large social circle, did I have trouble making friendships or did I never have the opportunity to make friends?

- Did I have strict or lenient parents?

- Was I spoiled as a child?

- Did I grow up rich or in an underprivileged family?

- What kind of child was I?

- What was my favorite thing to do as a child?

You may also talk to your parents, siblings, other family members, and childhood friends to gain more information. In addition, look at old family photo albums and videos, and notice what you wear, what you are doing in the pictures and who is with you in the pictures. The more you engage in childhood memories, the more you will remember and tap into the feelings you felt during a certain period of childhood.

Step two: Listen to your inner child

Now that you have connected to your inner child, it is time to listen to what it is saying. Find a method that works for you by using self-practices such as meditating or journaling. It is suggested that you schedule a specific time during your day to communicate with your inner child. Your method is the key to having access to unlocking deep traumas and information you need to become the adult version you were always meant to be.

The inner child is always communicating but we are not always all ears for many reasons. As adults, life always feels overwhelming with rare moments of being relaxed in which we often overlook the messages our inner child tries to communicate with us. Earlier it was mentioned that our inner child also surfaces when we feel unsafe and tend to feel triggered. In such moments, you may take a moment to step back, reflect and notice the message it is trying to tell you.

Below you will find an explanation of how to use a technique called visualization to communicate with your inner child.

Visualization is a form of meditation and uses similar steps meaning this technique won't be hard to try. Find a quiet and comfortable spot to do your visualization session and close your eyes. Then, visualize you at the age you suspect you experienced trauma followed by allowing the version of yourself you are visualizing to express pain and anger without feeling shame. Let the visualization of your younger self feel free to do whatever they desire to do in the moment. To enhance the experience of your visualization session, it is recommended that you also try your best to imagine the setting and some people who might be involved in the traumatic event you experienced.

Once you are able to see the younger version of yourself ask them some simple questions like:

- What emotion is the younger version of yourself feeling?
- What does the younger version of yourself need?
- What is the younger version of yourself blaming or shaming themselves for?

- What can you tell them as an attempt to comfort and support your younger self?

Note that the above questions do not need to be asked all at once, you can do one question per session. Your inner child will feel seen and heard by just asking one of those questions.

Step Three: Nurture, comfort and support your inner child

Step three is the final step that requires you to become the parent you never had. This is where you allow your adult self to provide your inner child with whatever it needs so that the adult self can thrive. During the first two years of being human we go through the first developmental stages proposed by Erikson called trust versus mistrust. If parents did not provide you with a sense of safety it led you to have trust issues and anxiety in which step three provides you with an opportunity to work on going back in time and letting the younger version of you know that it is okay to trust the world. Provide your younger self with an environment that feels safe as well as giving them unconditional love.

Here are two ways to provide you younger self with unconditional love and a sense of safety:

- The visualization technique introduced in step two — for step three you are asked to visualize giving your younger self physical affection such as holding them in your arms, caressing them gently, patting their back, or giving them a loving hug. In addition, deep down you know exactly what your inner child needs and how to comfort them therefore do not be afraid to follow your instincts and let the session flow as naturally as possible.

- Reinforcing positive self-talk and beliefs—this technique can be done in the mirror by using your eyes as a portal to access your inner child. You are the parent and the appearance you see in the mirror refers to your inner child. Tell the appearance in the mirror (the younger self) what you think they need to hear in that moment. Speak in a soft, soothing and loving tone as a parent would. Whatever you say to your younger self will have a powerful and healing effect.

NURTURING YOUR INNER CHILD

Addressing multiple letters to your inner child

Writing letters to yourself is a great way to connect, communicate and nurture the inner child. This is an opportunity to communicate your feelings, to let go of things you have always wanted to express and to heal. Write letters addressed to the adult version of you from the inner child and from the adult version of yourself to the inner child.

In the letter addressed to your adult self, you will allow the inner child to speak with no filter or boundaries. Remember, when we are young we are the most honest beings while being unaware that what we say can hurt the feelings of others. Be this person in your letter. Set the inner child free to express whatever they desire to share. Besides addressing this letter to the adult version of yourself, you can also write a letter to someone who triggered your inner child to feel unsafe for example, one of your parents, your partner or a friend. Whoever has hurt you, write a letter to them by letting them know the perspective of your inner child.

In the letters addressed to your inner child, be careful what you say. What you repeatedly say to the inner child will be internalized and will manifest consciously and subconsciously. Your letter should be comforting, validating and supporting the inner child as well as give them the things they didn't receive during childhood from a parent. Recognize that the inner child is suffering and experiencing pain, then try to empathize with them. If the inner child feels shame and guilt, tell them where it stems from and what causes them to feel pain. Next, you will let your inner child know that it was never their fault if parents failed at loving them in ways they needed as a child. As you write, inform the inner child that life will be different now that you have stepped into the parent role. Remind the inner child that how their pain surfaces in you as an adult will now change to more effective and healthier behaviors because you will guide them. Close your letter off by thanking your inner child, showing your love and reassuring them that you will always be with them.

Pretend to have a conversation with your inner child

This exercise is synonymous with the one explained in step three in which you speak to your reflection in the mirror. However, it can also be done without a mirror. Here is how to get started:

1. Identify the emotions of the inner child. Are they distressed, anxious, scared, or upset?

2. Provide the inner child with comforting words. Speak to your inner child the way it always wanted to be spoken to when they experienced a crisis during childhood. Figure out what the inner child needs to desperately hear and say it out loud to them.

3. Soothe their feelings in order for the adult version of you to find peace and to evolve into a better version of yourself.

4. An extra tip: Meditate to continue connecting with your inner child. Also, you can use guided meditations found on the internet to help you have a successful meditation session.

Write in your journal as the inner child and as the parent

When you write in your journal as the inner child, write with the hand that you are nondominant. In this way, you gain access to the right side of the brain that controls intuition and emotional expressions (Ford, 2021). The nondominant hand reflects the inner child who is still learning to navigate life, and feels inferior but has a fresh perspective of the world.

Write with the nondominant hand when the inner child gets an opportunity to communicate and respond to the inner child with the dominant hand to reflect the parent role (adult version of you). The nondominant hand will express feelings and the dominant hand will write soothing words to calm the inner child's spirit. According to Ford (2021), with this distinct separation in dialogue, your mind will be able to associate the exercise as an actual conversation between two halves of yourself working together to heal and understand each other. Conversations between you and your inner child should consist of empathy and compassion.

Allow the inner child to surface through being creative

Find an artistic activity to allow your creative side to awaken. There are many ways to do this exercise such as drawing, singing, dancing, playing an instrument and so forth. Try to remember which activities made you the happiest as a child and attempt them again. This is an exercise that nurtures the inner child through allowing them to feel free to express themselves through art. You will be surprised how singing and dancing can act as a release to inner turmoil your younger self might be experiencing. Also, drawing and painting can help you as the adult version to find more messages from your inner child.

Make time to play

As an adult this might sound odd, but right now you are catering to your inner child. Which activity could you do as a child and never get tired of? Whether it was building puzzles, reading, or rollerblading outside, do it again. Let the inner child come out to play and make sure the adult version is also participating. Ford (2021) recommends that you should respond to the inner child's playfulness, and allow its lightheartedness, curiosity, and tenderness to react through you.

Make a list of all the cartoons you watched and add to the movies and books you have read as a child. Rewatch one of your favorite shows/movies as a child or read a book you enjoyed back then. In addition, the process of reparenting isn't all about doing the hard work, in this part of reparenting the inner child you will allow yourself to have fun. Set up a playdate with your inner child and go to an amusement park, arcade, or roll in the grass. One thing about adults, we always enjoy engaging in activities that are meant for younger children (for example, playing in a bounce house).

Note: Don't judge your inner child for the things they enjoy, and don't feel childish for engaging in these activities as an adult.

You may ask, why go through all this effort, and how will it benefit me? Well, reparenting can help with a range of problems you experience as a narcissist such as self-sabotage, dealing with abuse, abandonment issues, anger management problems and relationship difficulties. This is how reparenting will improve your narcissistic personality:

- You create a portal to gain access to memories you have repressed as a child which kept you stuck in a particular developmental stage.

- You will gain confidence, self-belief and the ability to set boundaries and well to respect the boundaries of others.

- Your level of self-love and self-awareness will increase.

- You will be able to cater for yourself in ways you always needed to but never had the tools to do so.

- You will start being more compassionate toward yourself and others.

- You will learn to have fun and to cultivate healthy relationships.

AFTERWORD

How to Stop Being a Narcissist fed you with a large amount of information. In this book, five techniques to improve your narcissistic personality were discussed. Each step left you with ample knowledge to apply to your life, but taking action is now in your hands. Now that you know the theory, it is time to take control of your life by pushing your narcissistic tendencies to the side, improving yourself, and mending your relationships.

Let's look at a recap with some of the main key points of this book. Chapter 1 covered everything you needed to know about narcissism. You learned about the two different types of narcissists, grandiose and vulnerable narcissism, as well as narcissistic personality disorder. Another aspect of narcissism you learned was whether you have healthy narcissism, unhealthy, or pathological. The first chapter provided you with information that gave you an opportunity to self-diagnose by stating the signs of grandiose and vulnerable narcissism and the DSM-5 criteria of narcissistic personality disorder. Furthermore, we discussed the various causes of narcissism as we learned that there is not only one factor that could contribute to the development of narcissistic personality. Factors we looked at were temperament, parenting styles, genetics, the social world, and brain structure. Lastly, chapter 1 told you there is no cure for narcissistic personality disorder, but it can be improved by applying the techniques discussed in this book. The main point of chapter 1 was to identify where on the narcissistic spectrum you fall.

Chapter 2 focused on the first strategy that kicked off your healing journey. It encourages you to implement mindfulness practices in your life. Most articles stated that mindfulness can contribute to an individual's narcissism because being mindful means you go within, and the practice is solely focused on you. However, it is a useful tool if you use it correctly. The main idea of doing mindfulness practices is to raise your level of awareness and to gain insight around your personality issue. This is an important part of your healing journey because as a narcissist, you have difficulty doing introspection and admitting when you have been wrong. Therefore, in a mindfulness session, you will have a mental space to reflect on your behavior toward yourself and others. In this moment, you can be still and analyze how your personality negatively affects your life. The second part of chapter 2 discussed six ways how mindfulness improves narcissistic tendencies: It challenges the stories you tell about yourself and the world around you, helps you create an optimal and healthy level of self-confidence, changes the belief that you are better than the rest, increases your level of self-awareness, makes you aware that you do things to please others, and decreases the impact of trauma experienced as a result of having a narcissistic parent. Next, you learned three popular ways of practicing mindfulness: namely, doing a body scan, sitting, and walking meditation. You also learned that your narcissistic traits can be treated as a habit, because your automatic responses have developed in the same way as habits are formed. Four easy steps were named and explained to break narcissistic habits followed by six steps to make mindfulness a habit. Lastly, you learned that mindfulness has eight benefits that will improve narcissistic tendencies.

Chapter 3 motivated you to be grateful and to practice gratitude. Narcissists are well-known for being self-absorbed and wanting to have all the attention on them, in which they refuse to acknowledge how external sources improve their lives. This may be a result of excessive praise from parents as well as being spoiled. The normal reality for you might have been receiving everything you want, and now as an adult you expect this treatment from the world. This chapter needed you to unlearn the expectations you have when you go out into the world, socializing, working and forming relationships with others. In order to unlearn those irrational expectations from others, it was suggested that you show gratitude whenever someone is showing you kindness. There could be one of two causes that formed these expectations: the first cause refers to a child who was excessively spoiled and the second cause states that strict parents who kept their children away from the world created a child lacking basic social skills. Chapter 3 stated that narcissists do not have the capacity to express gratitude toward anything or anyone, but it does teach them how to make gratitude a habit and a natural part of their personality. The chapter encourages you to see the silver lining, and to acknowledge that one's success does not only come from yourself but many external factors. Next, you were taught various ways to practice gratitude on a daily basis (for example, naming five aspects you are grateful for, or choosing someone new every week to be grateful for such as your mother, partner, colleague, etc.). Because you lack social skills, you were informed about saying thank you and apologizing sincerely. The last section of the chapter discussed how practicing gratitude will improve narcissistic tendencies.

Narcissists are obsessed with themselves and fixate on certain parts of them whether it is their appearance, materialistic things they own and their successful careers. Chapter 4's strategy had a main goal of helping you redirect the attention from yourself to the external world. Instead of wanting to have attention on you 24/7, leaving no room for other things or people to be in the limelight. You are encouraged in this chapter to consciously pay attention to the outside world. This chapter taught you how to be less self-absorbed, not to seek approval from everyone you know and to show a genuine interest in others. Next, we looked at being self-compassionate instead of boasting about what you have and who you are through self-promotion. Grandiose narcissists love to broadcast their lives while vulnerable narcissists are not the kind of person to be boastful. Being compassionate means being sympathetic toward others and giving yourself love and kindness even in times when you fail, feel like life's falling apart or lack hope, etc. In three steps, you learned to be a compassionate person. The following part of chapter 4 motivated you to keep your eyes on the main purpose of life. Why are you part of this world; what's your job on this earth? We may all have different purposes and choose to live our purpose differently, but it all points back to one purpose called love. Love heals and conquers all. You may believe that the job you chose to do is to fill your pockets or to provide you with a life that will make others envy you. However, if you change your mindset, you will realize the reason why you devoted your life to a specific career is because you want to provide a service to others. At the end, you were reminded to make use of six steps to stay focused on your purpose.

Chapter 5 dealt with the famous and most used therapy, cognitive behavioral therapy. The main key points of this chapter refers to the various techniques you were provided with that could be done without a professional mental health practitioner. The techniques discussed such as cognitive reframing, behavioral activation, behavioral experiments, journaling and using thought records, and lastly, strengthening some of your skills to be better equipped on your journey ahead. These skills refer to social and communication skills as narcissists lack making use of social rules. The first technique we looked at was cognitive restructuring in which it aims to help you restructure distorted and irrational thinking patterns. We also explained a few cognitive distortions in order to better understand narcissistic behaviors.

The final chapter discusses reparenting the inner child. This chapter makes you dig deep in your past to uncover traumas or any problems the inner child might be experiencing because only then can the adult personality start developing. The trauma you experienced kept you stuck in a particular developmental stage. Reparenting yourself may sound odd but it only requires the adult version of yourself to provide TLC to the inner child. The key points of the last chapter are the three steps of reparenting the inner child: connecting, communicating and nurturing the younger version of the self. Lastly, reparenting the inner child is a challenging process, but it also involves having fun.

To conclude, you are the only one who can decide which direction your life goes. You have the power to change and to heal your relationships. However, you need to realize you shouldn't only heal in isolation. Yes, you have the knowledge and you are doing the inner work, but healing can only be successful once you apply these techniques to real life situations. If you have been distancing yourself from relationships in order to heal, for example, the real healing work starts when you feel ready to connect with people again.

REFERENCES

Ackerman, C. E. (2017). *28 Benefits of Gratitude & Most Significant Research Findings.* Positive Psychology. https://positivepsychology.com/benefits-gratitude-research-questions/

Allen, S. (n.d.). *Why Is Gratitude So Hard for Some People?* Gratefulness. https://gratefulness.org/resource/why-is-gratitude-so-hard-for-some-people/

Altered brain structure in pathological narcissism. (2013). Science Daily. https://www.sciencedaily.com/releases/2013/06/130619101434.htm

Ankrom, S. (2022). *8 Deep Breathing Exercises for Anxiety.* Verywellmind. https://www.verywellmind.com/abdominal-breathing-2584115

Aster, H. (2021). *6 Tips for Staying Focused on Your Purpose.* Short Form. https://www.shortform.com/blog/focus-on-your-purpose/

Barlow, D. H., Durand, V. M., du Plessis, L. M., & Visser, C. (2017). *Abnormal Psychology: An Integrative Approach, 1st South African edition.* Cengage Learning.

Bartosch, J. (2020). *Study shows Narcissistic Personality Disorder may have a biological component.* UChicago Medicine. https://www.uchicagomedicine.org/forefront/research-and-discoveries-articles/study-shows-narcissistic-personality-disorder-may-have-a-biological-component#:~:text=A%20study%20led%20by%20University,also%20connected%20to%20interpersonal%20hypersensitivity.

Behary, W. (2013). *Why Are Narcissists So Hard to Treat?* Psychotherapy Networker. https://www.psychotherapynetworker.org/blog/details/749/why-are-narcissists-so-hard-to-treat

Brogaard, B. (2019). *Vulnerable Vs Grandiose Narcissism: Which Is More Harmful.* Psychology Today. https://www.psychologytoday.com/za/blog/the-mysteries-love/201906/vulnerable-vs-grandiose-narcissism-which-is-more-harmful

Carpenter, D. (n.d.). *The Science Behind Gratitude (and How It Can Change Your Life).* Happify Daily. https://www.happify.com/hd/the-science-behind-gratitude/

Chen, S. (2018). *Give Yourself a Break: The Power of Self-Compassion.* Harvard Business Review. https://hbr.org/2018/09/give-yourself-a-break-the-power-of-self-compassion

Cherry, K. (2021). *What Is Gratitude?* Verywellmind. https://www.verywellmind.com/what-is-gratitude-5206817

Cognitive-Behavioral Therapy for Personality Disorders (CBT). (n.d.). MentalHelp.net. https://www.mentalhelp.net/personality-disorders/cognitive-behavioral-therapy/#:~:text=CBT%20is%20particularly%20helpful%20for,patterns%20are%20exposed%20and%20challenged.

Cognitive Behavior Therapy Techniques. (n.d.). Cognitive Behavioral Therapy Los Angeles. https://cogbtherapy.com/cognitive-behavior-therapy-techniques

Davis, S. (2020). *Reparenting to Heal the Wounded Inner Child.* cptsdfoundation.org. https://cptsdfoundation.org/2020/07/27/reparenting-to-heal-the-wounded-inner-child/

Dempsey, K. (n.d.). *How To Spot A Vulnerable Narcissist.* the awareness centre. https://theawarenesscentre.com/vulnerable-narcissist/

Edberg, H. (2021). *Focus Outward to Win Friends and Improve your People Skills*. The Positivity Blog. https://www.positivityblog.com/focus-outward-to-win-friends-and-improve-your-people-skills/

Emmons, R. (2013). *What Gets in the Way of Gratitude?* Greater Good Magazine. https://greatergood.berkeley.edu/article/item/what_stops_gratitude

Epstein, M. (1986). Meditative Transformations of Narcissism. *The Journal of Transpersonal Psychology, 18*(2), 143-158. https://www.atpweb.org/jtparchive/trps-18-86-02-143.pdf

Excellence Reporter. (2019). Ralph Waldo Emerson: On Love, Beauty and the Purpose of Life. Excellence Reporter. https://excellencereporter.com/2019/02/18/ralph-waldo-emerson-on-love-beauty-and-the-purpose-of-life/

Fishman, S. (2021). *Is Narcissism Treatable?* HealthGrades. https://www.healthgrades.com/right-care/mental-health-and-behavior/is-narcissism-treatable

Ford, D. (2021). *Reparenting Your Inner Child: Ways to Encourage Therapeutic Dialogue*. Step Up For Mental Health. https://www.stepupformentalhealth.org/reparenting-your-inner-child/

Fulton, B. (2020). *The Benefits of Gratitude and How to Get Started*. Healthline. https://www.healthline.com/health/benefits-of-gratitude-practice

Gregory, C., & Soriano, K. (2022). *Tell Me All I Need to Know About Narcissistic Personality Disorder*. Psycom. https://www.psycom.net/personality-disorders/narcissistic/

Grohol, J. M. (2018). *The Difference Between Narcissism & Narcissistic Personality Disorder*. PsychCentral. https://psychcentral.com/blog/the-difference-between-narcissism-narcissistic-personality-disorder#1

How to Change Your Habits with Mindfulness. (n.d.). Mindful. https://www.mindful.org/how-to-change-your-habits-with-mindfulness/

How to say "sorry" and mean it. (n.d.). Reach Out.com. https://au.reachout.com/articles/how-to-say-sorry-and-mean-it

How To Use Behavioral Experiments To Test What You Believe. (n.d.). Psychology Tools. https://www.psychologytools.com/self-help/behavioral-experiments/

Inner Child Work: How to Heal By Reparenting Yourself. (n.d.). Big Self School. https://www.bigselfschool.com/post/inner-child-work

Jacobson, S. (2017). *Inner Child Work – What Is It and Can You Benefit?* Harley Therapy Counselling Blog. https://www.harleytherapy.co.uk/counselling/inner-child-work-can-benefit.htm#:~:text=The%20general%20idea%20of%20inner,talking%29%20with%20your%20inner%20child

Jamgochian, J. (n.d.). *When To Say "I'm Sorry" And When To Say "Thank You"*. Hartstein Psychological Services. https://www.hartsteinpsychological.com/when-to-say-sorry-or-thank-you

Lascala, M. (2021). *30+ Inspiring Quotes About Change, Because We Never Stop Evolving*. GH. https://www.goodhousekeeping.com/life/g25383377/quotes-about-change/?slide=1

Mancao, A. (2020). *Not Every Person With Narcissistic Traits Has Narcissistic Personality Disorder*. mbglifestyle. https://www.mindbodygreen.com/articles/not-every-narcissist-has-narcissistic-personality-disorder/

Martinez, W., & Alayan, A. (2021). *The Psychology of Purpose in Life*. Colorado State University. https://www.research.colostate.edu/healthyagingcenter/2021/07/13/the-psychology-of-purpose-in-life/

Matusiewicz, A. K., Hopwood, C. J., Banducci, A. N., & Lejuez, C.W. (2010). The Effectiveness of Cognitive Behavioral Therapy for Personality Disorders. *Psychiatric Clinics of North America, 33*(3), 657-685. https://www.ncbi.nlm.nih.gov/pmc/articles/PMC3138327/

Mayo Clinic Staff. (n.d.). *Cognitive behavioral therapy*. Mayo Clinic. https://www.mayoclinic.org/tests-procedures/cognitive-behavioral-therapy/about/pac-20384610

Mayo Clinic Staff. (2020). *Mindfulness exercises*. Mayo Clinic.
https://www.mayoclinic.org/healthy-lifestyle/consumer-health/in-
depth/mindfulness-exercises/art-20046356

Mayor Galindo, P. C. (2021). *What is gratitude? 5 ways to be thankful*.
https://www.betterup.com/blog/gratitude-definition-how-to-practice

Mindful Staff. (2020). *What is Mindfulness?* Mindful. https://www.mindful.org/what-is-
mindfulness/

Mind Tools Content Team. (n.d.). *Cognitive Restructuring Reducing Stress by Changing Your
Thinking*. mindtools. https://www.mindtools.com/pages/article/newTCS_81.htm

Morin, A. (2014). *7 Scientifically Proven Benefits Of Gratitude That Will Motivate You To Give
Thanks Year-Round*. Forbes. https://www.forbes.com/sites/amymorin/2014/11/23/7-
scientifically-proven-benefits-of-gratitude-that-will-motivate-you-to-give-thanks-
year-round/?sh=2fd75793183c

Morin, A. (2020). *How to Perform Behavioral Experiments Test how real your assumptions are
and you might change your life*. Verywellmind.
https://www.verywellmind.com/how-to-perform-behavioral-experiments-4779864

Passfield, R. (2019). *Mindfulness: An Antidote to Narcissism*. Grow Mindfulness.
https://growmindfulness.com/mindfulness-an-antidote-to-
narcissism/#:~:text=Mindfulness%20meditation%2C%20in%20its%20many,awaren
ess%20and%20improved%20self%2Dmanagement.

Patterson, E. (2021). *What Is Grandiose Narcissism?* Choosing Therapy.
https://www.choosingtherapy.com/grandiose-narcissism/

Pedersen, T. (2021). *What Causes Narcissistic Personality Disorder?* PsychCentral.
https://psychcentral.com/disorders/what-causes-narcissistic-personality-disorder

Pietrangelo, A. (2020). *How to Treat Narcissistic Personality Disorder*. Healthline.
https://www.healthline.com/health/therapy-for-narcissism

Raypole, C. (2020). *Can Narcissistic People Change?* Healthline.
https://www.healthline.com/health/can-a-narcissist-change

Raypole, C. (2021). *8 Ways to Start Healing Your Inner Child*. Healthline.
https://www.healthline.com/health/mental-health/inner-child-healing

Robinson, F. (2022). *8 Highly Effective Ways To Stop Being Self-Centered*. A Conscious
Rethink. https://www.aconsciousrethink.com/18176/how-to-stop-being-self-
centered/

Saeed, K. (2019). *Can Narcissism Be Cured? Too Many Tricksters Are Providing False
Claims*. PsychCentral. https://psychcentral.com/blog/liberation/2019/01/can-
narcissism-be-cured-too-many-tricksters-are-providing-false-claims

Saunderson, R. (2017). *How To Say Thank You Like You Mean It*. Authentic Recognition.
https://authenticrecognition.com/how-to-say-thank-you-like-you-really-mean-
it/#:~:text=Speak%20clearly%20as%20you%20give,saying%20thank%20you%20to
%20people.

Saxena, S. (2021). *What is a Vulnerable Narcissist? Signs, Causes, & How to Deal With One*.
Choosingtherapy. https://www.choosingtherapy.com/vulnerable-narcissist/

Shaw, E. (2019). *The Narcissist Believes Only What They Want To Believe, Cognitive
Distortions*. https://wasitme.blog/2019/10/17/the-narcissist-believes-what-only-they-
want-to-believe-cognitive-distortions/

TheraNest Team. (2020). *Top Cognitive Behavioral Therapy Techniques*. TheraNest.
https://theranest.com/blog/top-cognitive-behavioral-therapy-techniques/

Treating Narcissistic Personality Disorder With CBT. (2015). Avalon Malibu.
https://www.avalonmalibu.com/blog/treating-narcissistic-personality-disorder-with-
cbt/

Vaknin, S. (2009). *The Narcissistic Patient - A Case Study*. HealthyPlace.
https://www.healthyplace.com/personality-disorders/malignant-self-
love/narcissistic-patient-a-case-study

Villines, Z. (2021). *What is behavioral activation?* Medical News Today.
https://www.medicalnewstoday.com/articles/behavioral-activation

WebMD Editorial Contributors. (2020). *Narcissism: Symptoms and Signs*. WebMD. https://www.webmd.com/mental-health/narcissism-symptoms-signs

WebMD Editorial Contributors. (2020). *Narcissism: Symptoms and Signs*. WebMD. https://www.webmd.com/mental-health/narcissism-symptoms-signs#:~:text=Those%20with%20grandiose%20narcissism%20are,behavior%20are%20much%20more%20sensitive.

What Are The Benefits Of Cognitive Behaviour Therapy (CBT)? (2019). my life psychologists. https://mylifepsychologists.com.au/what-are-the-benefits-of-cognitive-behaviour-therapy-cbt/

What is Cognitive Behavioral Therapy? (2017). Clinical Practice Guideline for the Treatment of Post Traumatic Stress Disorder. https://www.apa.org/ptsd-guideline/patients-and-families/cognitive-behavioral

What Is Purpose? (n.d.). Greater Good Magazine. https://greatergood.berkeley.edu/topic/purpose/definition#what-is-purpose

Why Practice It? (n.d.). Greater Good Magazine. https://greatergood.berkeley.edu/topic/mindfulness/definition#why-practice-mindfulness

Wilding, M. (2018). *I'm a professor of human behaviour, and I have some news for you about the 'narcissists' in your life*. Business insider. https://www.businessinsider.co.za/narcissism-vs-narcissist-2018-11?r=US&IR=T

Wright, K., & Furnham, A. (2014). What Is Narcissistic Personality Disorder? Lay Theories of Narcissism. *Psychology*, *5*(9), 1120-1130. https://www.scirp.org/html/15-6901195_48298.htm

Zajenkowski, M., Maciantowicz, O., Szymaniak, K., & Urban, P. (n.d.). Vulnerable and Grandiose Narcissism Are Differentially Associated With Ability and Trait Emotional Intelligence. *Frontiers in Psychology*, *9*(1606). https://www.frontiersin.org/articles/10.3389/fpsyg.2018.01606/full

Ziogas, G. J. (2021). *How to Be Less Self-Centered and More Community-Focused*. Medium. https://medium.com/personal-growth/how-to-be-less-self-centered-and-more-community-focused-7428637d1dda

9 798215 024843